THE TRANSCENDENT UNITY OF RELIGIONS

the text of this book is printed
on 100% recycled paper

FRITHJOF SCHUON

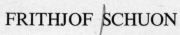

The Transcendent Unity

of Religions

Translated by PETER TOWNSEND

REVISED EDITION

Introduction by HUSTON SMITH

HARPER TORCHBOOKS

Harper & Row, Publishers

New York, Evanston, San Francisco, London

First published as DE L'UNITÉ TRANSCENDANTE DES RELIGIONS © Editions
Gallimard 1948

First HARPER TORCHBOOK edition published 1975

LIBRARY OF CONGRESS CATALOG CARD NUMBER: 74–9137

STANDARD BOOK NUMBER: 06–139415–7

Designed by Stephanie Krasnow

Spiritus ubi vult spirat: et vocem eius audis, sed nescis unde veniat, aut quo vadat: sic est omnis, qui natus est ex spiritu.

The wind bloweth where it listeth, and thou hearest the sound thereof, but canst not tell whence it cometh, and whither it goeth: so is every one that is born of the Spirit.

John 3:8

Contents

Introduction to the Revised Edition

by Huston Smith

Of the first edition of this book, published in 1957, T. S. Eliot wrote: "I have met with no more impressive work in the comparative study of Oriental and Occidental religions." As I would myself raise his estimate to the superlative, one wonders why the book is not better known. The subtlety of its arguments cannot be the sole reason; there appears to be something about Schuon's entire approach to the relation between religions that, being foreign to the contemporary theological scene—a way of saying "original"—renders it peculiarly difficult of access. Instead of locking into the ongoing dialogue on the subject—names like Schleiermacher, Troeltsch, Barth, Brunner, Tillich, Hans Kung and Wilfred Smith never appear on his pages—he approaches it from a different angle, a distinctive bent. Until this angle is perceived, his entire perspective is likely to seem askew; thereafter it falls into place. It then emerges as at once the most powerful statement of the grand, or better, primordial, tradition to appear in modern times and a statement of that tradition that is original in incorporating what our age for the first time demands: that religion be treated in global terms.

I was myself baffled by the book on first round, with the consequence that it sat half-read on my shelves for a decade until a curious sequence of events opened me to its thesis. It was the autumn of 1969, and I was embarking on an academic year around the world. Of the decisions as to what to include in my forty-four-pound luggage limit, the final one concerned a book that had just crossed my desk: *In the Tracks of Buddhism,* by Frithjof Schuon. My indifference to his earlier book made it seem clearly expendable, but its middle section, entitled "Buddhism's Ally in Japan: Shinto or the Way of the Gods," caught my eye. Two weeks hence, at our first stop, Japan, I would have to lecture on Shinto and I had little feel for its outlook. I badly needed an entrée, and more in desperation than in hope, I wedged the book into my bulging flight bag.

It proved to be the best decision of the year. Before the sacred shrine at Ise, symbolic center of the nation of Japan, under its giant cryptomeria and at low tables in its resthouse for pilgrims, the Way of the Gods opened before me. Ise's atmosphere itself could be credited with the unveiling, but only if I add that it was Schuon's insights that enabled me to sense within that atmosphere —its dignity, beauty, and repose—an intellective depth. I came to see how ancestors could appear less fallen than their descendants and thereby serve, when revered, as doorways to transcendence. I saw how virgin nature—especially in its grand phenomena: sun, wind, moon, thunder, lightning, and the sky and earth that are their containers—could be venerated as the most transparent symbols of the divine. Above all, I saw how Shinto, indigenous host for "the Japanese miracle," could be seen as the most intact instance of an archaic hyperborean shamanism that swept from Siberia across the Bering Straits to the red Indians of America.

Two months later, in India, the same thing happened. Perusing a bookstore in Madras, my eye fell on a study of the Vedanta entitled *Language of the Self,* again by Frithjof Schuon. This time I didn't hesitate; the remaining weeks in India were spent with that book under my arm, and I was happy. A decade's tutelage under a swami of the Ramakrishna Order had familiarized me with Vedanta's basic outlook, but Schuon took off from there as from base camp, while showing at each step, through a stunning series of cross-references, how the Vedantic profundities being treated were Indic variations on themes that are universal because grounded in man's inherent nature as related to his Source.

Would one believe a third installment? In Iran the leading Islamicist of the land pointed me to Schuon's *Understanding Islam* as "the best work in English on the meaning of Islam and why Muslims believe in it."

I had been to East Asia, South Asia, and West Asia, and in each the same personage had surfaced to guide and illumine. Here was someone doing what I had myself been trying to do, but doing it at a level of competence that differed not in degree but in kind. Needless to say, on returning home I reached for his original book, the one here reissued, with new interest. And with new eyes. The overview was as impressive as the individual studies that had schooled me for it.

As other readers cannot be expected to have undergone that schooling, I propose in this introduction to do two things by way of propaedeutics: to summarize the author's thesis and to relate it to alternatives that are being proposed.

1. The Relation between Religions: Schuon's Thesis

The Essence/Accident Distinction in Religions

It is a priori evident that everything both resembles and differs from everything else: resembles it at least in existing, differs or there would be no multiplicity to compare. *Pari passu* with religions: had they nothing in common we would not refer to them by a common noun; were they undifferentiated we would not speak of them in the plural and the noun would be proper. Everything turns on how this empty truth is filled with content. Where is the line between unity and plurality to be drawn and how are the two domains to be related?

Schuon's Version of the Essence/Accident Distinction: Esoteric versus Exoteric

Schuon draws the line between esoteric and exoteric. And immediately we begin to suspect that we are in the presence of something different. The fundamental distinction is not between religions; it is not, so to speak, a line that, reappearing, divides religion's great historical manifestations vertically, Hindus from Buddhists from Christians from Muslims, and so on. The dividing line is horizontal and occurs but once, cutting across the historical religions. Above the line lies esoterism, below it exoterism.

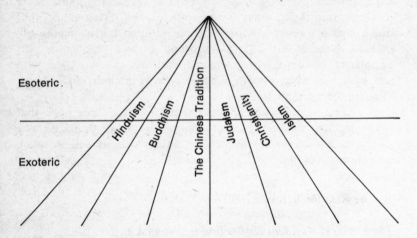

It could be objected that this horizontal line is not as original as it might appear; the thesis that religions are alike at heart or in essence (read "esoterically") while differing in form ("exoterically") has often been advanced. The point is well taken; we do not arrive at Schuon's originality until we ask into the nature of religion's generic essence or (in the title of this book) transcendent unity.

For Schuon existence is graded, and with it cognition as well. Metaphysically, in God at the apex, religions (or rather the revealed religions, a distinction to which we shall return) converge;* below they differ. The epistemological concomitant of this metaphysical fact is that religious discernment, too, unites at its apex while dividing below it.†

* "That they all may be one . . . in Thee" (John, 18:21).

† This distinction of levels is fundamental; without it confusion is inevitable. Here is a sample: in the introduction to *Attitudes toward Other Religions,* ed., Owen Thomas (New York: Harper & Row, 1969), we read:

Our objector could protest that we still have not been taken beyond the essence-unity/accident-diversity framework, for no one claims that the unity posited in this framework is evident to everyone. Again the point is in order and it presses us to specify what for Schuon is the nature of the requisite discernment and what appears to it.

What appears to it is Unity: absolute, categorical, undifferentiated Unity. Anthropologically this Unity precludes final distinction between human and divine, epistemologically between knower and known. It bespeaks a knowing that becomes its object, or rather is its object, for temporal distinctions are likewise inapposite at this point.

This should get us past the notion that Schuon's version of the essence/accident distinction is run of the mill. From his perspective the defect in other versions of this distinction is that they claim unity in religions too soon, at levels where, being exoteric, true Unity does not pertain and can be posited only on pain of Procrusteanism or vapidity.

The Absolute Unity that is God defies visualization or even consistent description, but is nonetheless required, for in the symbolism of the spirit the separation on which duality rides tokens ignorance epistemologically and privation affectively. The Unity must, however, be of an exceptional, indeed unique, kind, for it must include everything; if anything possessed reality apart from it, this would reintroduce the division that Absolute Unity by definition precludes. Absolute Unity must be All-Possibility: every possibility must be actualized within it—with God in his personal mode all things are possible (Matt. 19:26; Mark 10:27); in his absolute mode all things are actual. Man's mind cannot imagine a Something that excludes nothing save distinctions, any more than it can

---

"It is sometimes asserted that all religions are equally true. But this would seem to be simply sloppy thinking, since the various religions hold views of reality which are sharply different if not contradictory" (p. 20). To cite an analogy Schuon himself invokes, if *A* sees a red light and *B* one that is blue, it is not sloppy thinking to assert that both are seeing light. The same point applies to the statement that appears on the page following the one just quoted: "What is really true for us must be universally true, for that is what truth means."

visualize light that is simultaneously wave and particle, electrons that jump orbit without traversing the intervening space, or a particle that travels alternate paths simultaneously without dividing. Physics transcends the paradoxes nature poses for human imagery and the ordinary language that derives from it by means of mathematics: nature cannot be consistently imaged, but it can be consistently conceived, through equations. Metaphysics in the etymological meaning of that which lies "after" or beyond *physis,* or nature, transcends by means of the Intellect the parallel paradoxes that Reality poses for language and visualization.

The Intellect is not reason. Reason proceeds discursively, through language, and like a bridge, joins two banks, knower and known, without removing the river between. The Intellect knows intuitively and (as noted above) identifies the knower with what he knows, causing one to become the other.* Or rather, to invoke again the point about time, the Intellect *is* the Absolute as manifest in the human soul; Eckhart states the case precisely when he writes: "There is something in the soul that is uncreated and uncreatable; . . . this something is the Intellect." What appears from mundane perspective as the Intellect coming to know the Absolute is in actuality the Intellect as Absolute-in-man becoming perceptible to phenomenal awareness.† Atman is Brahman from the beginning. "Wonder of wonders, all things intrinsically *are* the Buddha-nature."

The Esoteric/Exoteric Distinction as Deriving from Spiritual Types

Intimations and realizations of this supreme identity appear in varying degrees of explicitness in all revealed religions and constitute the point at which they are one. But this establishes religious

---

* In Sanskrit one who knows in this mode is *evaṁvit,* a Comprehensor, one who has "verified" in his own person. As long as one knows only of his immortal Self, he is still in the realm of ignorance; he really knows it only when he becomes it.

† "In Shinran's teaching the so-called 'in the future' [when applied to man's deliverance] means, in reality, 'in the infinite depth of one's consciousness'" (Shojun Bando, "Significance of the Nembutsu," *Studies in Comparative Religion,* Autumn, 1972, p. 215).

unity on the esoteric plane; it is hidden and secret not because those who know will not tell, but because the truth to which they are privy is buried so deep in the human composite that they cannot communicate it, not in any way the majority will find convincing.* As the Intellect undercuts the world of distinctions, from the standpoint of discriminating perception that divides into subject and object, it appears nonexistent. So the issue of unity and diversity in religion is converted into one of spiritual types: esoteric and exoteric. The esoteric minority consists of men and women who realize that they have their roots in the Absolute. Either they experience the identification directly or, failing this, they stand within earshot of its claim; something within them senses that the claim is true even if they cannot validate it completely. The exoteric majority is composed of the remainder of mankind for whom this way of talking about religion is sterile if not unintelligible.

Ambivalence as the Attitude of Each toward the Other

The attitude of each spiritual type toward the other must in the nature of things be, at best, ambivalent. The esoteric will honor the exoteric's faith, for he will see it as invested in scripture and/or incarnation that truly are God's revelations. He will not, however, be able to share the exoteric's conviction that the text or life in which he encounters his revelation is the only, or in any event supreme, mode in which God has spoken. The exoteric's assessment of the esoteric is likely to be less charitable, not because exoterics are less endowed with that virtue, but because, a portion of the esoteric position being obscured from him, he cannot honor it without betraying the truth he does see. If, as the esoteric maintains, Revelation has multiple and equal instances, no single instance can be absolute. But single instance—be it Christ, the Koran, or whatever—is what the exoteric's faith is anchored in, so esoterism looms as exoterism's subverter. It is in this light that Christianty's ambivalence toward its mystics and Islam's toward

* "Those who say do not know; those who know do not say" (*Tao Tê Ching,* ch. 56).

its Sufis, to the point even of crucifying an Al-Ḥallāj, are to be understood.

Esoteric and Exoteric as Hierarchical

We are focusing on Schuon's notion of personality types as entrée to his understanding of the relation between religions, but the types he delineates are not on a par, like the Greeks' sanguine, choleric, phlegmatic, and bilious; Jung's extraverted and introverted, or his sensing, thinking, feeling, and intuiting types; or Sheldon's ectomorphs, endomorphs, and mesomorphs. They are graded, like Vedanta's sattvic (balanced), rajasic (dynamic), and tamasic (lethargic) characters. This returns us to the hierarchy of being, for if mankind admits of degrees, it is because being does; a hierarchy of worth arising out of a qualitatively undifferentiated, dead-level substrate is a superficial and ultimately contradictory image. Anthropology, ontology, and epistemology as well—all graded or none.

And once more we are struck by the originality in the contemporary West of Schuon's approach. Soon we shall be matching it against other voices on the relation between religions, but to anticipate, the central difference is that none of the others sets the problem in the context of degrees of being.

One wonders if anything separates the modern world from its predecessors more than its leveling of reality to a single dimension*

---

* The modern world does, of course, see *nature* as hierarchical, stretching from items measuring billionths of billionths of an inch to a universe twenty-eight billion light years across. From the metaphysical standpoint, however, this continuum is not hierarchical at all; it falls on a straight, horizontal line, the line of quantity as measured by size and strength of forces. The difference between the traditional and the modern world view comes to this: in the former, reality is as stupendous qualitatively as quantitatively, whereas the latter, while sharpening our understanding of the world's quantitative aspects, has collapsed its qualitative dimension to the distance between inanimate matter and human consciousness, a microspectrum when placed beside the *ens perfectissimum* in which the traditional world was anchored.

with, one is tempted to add, Marcuse's *One-Dimensional Man* as its inevitable corollary. Faithful to his incorrigible impression that certain disclosures were more profound than others, traditional man adduced the natural correlate that they activated a profounder mode of knowing that in turn carried him further into being than was normally the case.* The supposition is so natural† that one must ask why it has receded. The answer is not far to seek. Since the Great Chain of Being collapsed with the rise of modern science, something in scientific aims and methods must be inimical to it. It is. Modern science deals with the physical, perceptible world in that its hypotheses take off from this world and return to it for verification. As matter and perception (pointer readings, on/off flip-flops) are ultimately of a kind, differences in complexity and in the way matter behaves on different levels of size not being at issue here, the subject matter of science is one-dimensional. The modern world sees being as one-dimensional because scientific epistemology has pre-empted the epistemological field, not (one hastens to add) so much because scientists are imperialists as because humanists, certain theologians not excepted, have clamored to become satraps. The achievements of science make its take-over understandable, but this does not alter the fact that it is founded on a logical mistake, a kind of grand mistake whose consequences, conceptual and social, each is free to judge for himself.

---

* For the West, Plato forged the paradigm. The degrees of knowing are three. At bottom is opinion, or as we should say, observation. As this is constantly changing it grasps nothing permanent and worthy of being called "truth." The only knowledge fully deserving the name stands at the opposite end of the ladder; wholly transcending the senses, it is the contemplation by pure intelligence of the divine archetypes, above all the *sumum bonum,* the Idea of the Good. The overlap of these two modes of knowing, sensory and intellectual, results in an intermediate activity that Plato stigmatized as "bastard," though as a stepping stone to true knowledge it was invaluable. This middle "knowledge" was geometry, or as we should now say, deduction.

† "It has, in one form or another, been the dominant official philosophy of the larger part of civilized mankind through most of its history, [taught] in their several fashions and with differing degrees of rigor and thoroughness [by] the greater number of the subtler speculative minds and of the great religious teachers" (Arthur Lovejoy, *The Great Chain of Being: The History of an Idea* [New York: Harper & Brothers, 1960], p. 26).

2. Critique of Other Positions

Schuon will point out errors as he comes upon them, but he has no interest in elaborating a typology of the ways that the relationship between religions has been conceived; his eye is on the issue at stake rather than the ways men have construed it. I, on the other hand, do propose to sketch, in the balance of this introduction, a skeletal typology, to a double end. First, situating Schuon's thesis within it can etch that thesis more sharply; second, comparing his thesis with others may serve to feed it into the stream of ongoing discussion of the subject.

The continental divide that separates views on the relation between religions is the issue of commitment. The slopes on either side may be designated variously as existential versus objective, committed versus detached, or theological versus phenomenological; the three formulations are different ways of stating a single dichotomy.

The Theological, Committed Position

Rooted in theological conviction, the committed position necessarily concludes that the object of its commitment excels. In its baldest form it sees other commitments as evil opposed to its good, false as opposed to its truth. The invectives can be deserved. If the Old Testament inveighs against the surrounding paganism in categorical terms, it is because these nature religions had degenerated to the point where they had ceased to be saving *yanas* (vehicles) and deserved to be castigated. The epithet "false" is also appropriate when a faith that is valid in its own sphere bids to extend beyond that sphere into territory it could not incorporate salvifically; for the esoteric, it is in this light that Koranic objections to Judaism and Christianity are to be read. According to that perspective, the Koran does not deny the validity of these religions for their own adherents; it denies only that they were intended for—could save—the Arab world.

The true/false dichotomy forfeits its validity when invoked

against other revealed religions—"People of the Book"; roughly the great enduring religions and archaic ones that have not degenerated—in ways that are aggressive rather than defensive, that is, ways that deny dignity and legitimacy to other religions rather than defending these rights for one's own religion. With the exception of fundamentalists who disregard the specific targets to which the scriptural epithet "false" were directed and generalize the epithet to indict all faiths save the Christian, contemporary theologians concede that such blanket condemnations are indefensible. They are forced, however, to stop short of granting other revelations status equal to their own. Why forced? Because their faith (a) lodges in a particular revelation (b) from which other revelations differ. John is romantically in love with Mary; Jane is not Mary; John is not romantically in love with Jane. The twofold objection to this analogy is invalid. That Mary means the world to John, it might be argued, does not require John to deny that Susan can mean the world to Paul; but this overlooks the fact that "Lord of all" is ingredient to the concept of God whereas "beloved of all" is not ingredient to Mary. Second, to say that although John cannot love two women simultaneously romantically, he can love them simultaneously in other ways is to phase out of the analogy entirely, for as Kierkegaard put the matter, only the swain's love for the princess, that is, only romantic love by virtue of its all-consuming character and the way it sweeps out an entire world for the lover, can provide a paradigm for the love of God.

Denied the possibility of according full equality to other faiths, theology's compromise position—other religions contain some but lesser truth—has been formulated in several ways. In Christendom the classical formula has been "development-fulfillment": man's universal religious gropings find in Christ's incarnation of the Logos what they have sought implicitly from the beginning. Couched in terms of twentieth-century Biblical theologians' ruling concept of *Heilsgeschichte* (salvation history)—history as the field wherein God is working to accomplish his purpose of redeeming mankind—other religions are seen as valid responses to God's universal saving activity and thereby redeeming for their adherents without this prejudicing the fact that His most explicit, indeed decisive, redemptive act was in Christ. Karl Barth, architect of twentieth century neo-orthodoxy, pushed this view a step further. Building on Calvin's point that it is sin, man's rebellion, that prevents man from responding wholeheartedly to God's offer of salvation, he went on to argue that as sin is universal, Christianity must be distorted in the same way other religious responses are. By this analysis the divide is not between Christianity and other religions, but between the *kerygma* (divine message, God's saving overture) and religions' responses thereto, the Christian response included. But again the theological imperative that one's own revelation take precedence over others surfaces, here in the assumption that the *kerygma* is most decisively disclosed in Christ. When Bonhoeffer extrapolates from the sin-distorted character of religion generally to envision a "religionless Christianity," it continues to be assumed that Christianity is in the best position to perceive religion's self-seeking, and so to transcend it. Down the "religionless" road lies secular and death-of-God theology, but this *reductio ad absurdum*—the absurdity that man can discard religion before he discards his finitude—has to do with religion itself rather than the relationship between its instances, so it need not occupy us here.

The Objective, Detached Position

Whereas the foregoing position gauges the relation between religions through the eyes of a life involved in saving its soul, the objective, detached position—roughly the *Religionswissenschaft* of the last one hundred years—makes a point of having no commitment that might prejudice pure, impartial understanding. Not proceeding from within a religion, it approaches the field without presuming better or worse in its population. Some in this camp are nominalists and feel no compulsion to discover an essence that unifies the field; of religion in general they say as Troeltsch said of Christianity, it has no essence. The opposing camp of realists or essentialists divides into two subgroups. On the one hand stand reductionists who, being primarily interested in something other than religion, reduce religion to a manifestation or expression of this or that other entity: social reality (Durkheim), class struggle (Marx), ontogenetic development (Freud). Opposing them are the phenomenologists, whose slogan, "Let the phenomena (appearances) speak for themselves," was aimed precisely against reducing religion and certain other life domains to matrices that could only prove procrustean. Phenomenologists believe in religion's autonomy: man is inherently *Homo religiosus* and must be respected as such. All moves to explain why he is so in terms of other aspects of his existence dismantle his religiousness; in explaining it they explain it away and thereby falsify. Kant located the irreducibly religious in the moral imperative, Schleiermacher in man's feeling of absolute dependence, Rudolf Otto in his sense of the numinous. Today Eliade finds it in the dichotomy man erects between the sacred and the profane.

Note that these "essences" all fall on the human side of the God/man divide. Phenomena are not noumena. Phenomenology, trying to be a science, deals exclusively with the former and refrains in principle from pronouncing on trans-human, metaphysical entities.

The Search for a Compromise: The "Parliament of Religions" Approach

The two positions, theological and phenomenological, pull in opposite directions, and as each has a claim on something in man —were this not so they would not have arisen—leave him, as it were, with one foot on shore and the other on an unmoored craft. Ungainly at best, the stance is also precarious, so one could predict even before looking that efforts would be made to close the gap, to contrive a *via media* that retains the virtues of both positions (commitment and fair play) while eliminating their defects (prejudice and relativism). One can also see a priori the formal conditions a middle way must satisfy. First, it must center in something the great traditions have in common. But second, this something must be God-ward of the God/man divide, for attitudes, sentiments, and experiences, however lofty, are only human states and do not elicit worship: this silences phenomenology. By the same token, moral virtues cannot provide the common core, for though they may be common they are not the core. From the religious point of view ethics is always derivative: the ethical half of the Ten Commandments follows the theological half.

In the rationalism and deism of the seventeenth and eighteenth centuries, the Parliament of Religions (Chicago, 1893), Gilbert Reid's International Institute (Shanghai, 1894–1917), and the Temple of Understanding today, one sees earnest gropings to discover a theological core that religions share in common. What the endeavors are against is plain: the tragic and often contemptible prejudice, cresting at times into persecution, that can derive from religious alignments—the wars of religion that provoked Cardinal Newman's exclamation, "O how we hate one another for the love of God." But rebound from evils is not enough. Suppose we see the evils; what are we to do, relinquish religion or believe alike? As neither alternative is likely, the Parliament of Religions route brings us to an impasse as intractable as that between theology and phenomenology. As we have seen, the fact that the religions all endorse the Golden Rule isn't enough: men don't worship morality. If one moves beyond morality to archetypes—goodness, truth, and beauty—these too are common to the religions, but they fall between the stools: to the exoteric they appear abstract and no more capable of inspiring devotion than "womanhood" can trigger full-blown love, while to the esoteric they are not ultimate, but derive from a source beyond themselves to which they point. Beyond the archetypes exoterics cannot proceed in concert, for on the next echelon stands God in his immanent, in-formed, and personal mode, which mode has been differently disclosed to accommodate the differing characters and needs of the various civilizations.

Schuon's Alternative

Enter Schuon. There is a unity at the heart of religions. More than moral it is theological, but more than theological it is metaphysical in the precise sense of the word earlier noted: that which transcends the manifest world. The fact that it is thus transcendent, however, means that it can be univocally described by none and concretely apprehended by few. For these few the problem of the relation between religions is, by it, solved; for the many the problem is unsolvable, because for the many the generic is abstract and the concrete is not generic,* and only what is concrete can be loved and worshipped (this last holds for everyone).

Cut-Flower Esoterism

For positions on the relationship between religions we now have before us the theological, the phenomenological, the parliament-of-religions' unsuccessful effort to discover a common exoteric essence, and Schuon's transcendent unity. A final position, which I shall call cut-flower esoterism, will complete the typology.

Our times are witnessing an efflorescence of esoterism, but largely of a rootless variety. Unconvinced by theology, which along with theory of every sort is dismissed as a "head trip," the young especially are looking for experience: direct, unmediated God-awareness through altered states of consciousness. For Schuon this amounts to asking for end without means, kernel without husk, soul without body, spirit without letter. But as man is by definition finite as well as infinite, body as well as soul, this one-sided approach holds little promise. Short of being a *jivanmukta* (realized soul), so few of which exist as to be negligible in this context, man cannot keep God-realization in constant focus, and the way to keep it in focus as much as possible is through dedicated and faith-filled observance of the forms stipulated in one of the revealed traditions. The tradition's codes help to establish the soul in equilibrium socially and thereby emotionally, while theology provides a road map to point the direction and show where desert stretches

* Aristotle spoke for the many in this regard and in so doing effected, against his teacher Plato, the basic divide in Western philosophy. For Plato forms were concrete and existed in their own right; for Aristotle they existed only as aspects of materialized objects. Correlatively, for Plato the infinite was real, whereas for Aristotle it was a potentiality. Thus Aristotelianism may be regarded as a kind of external or exoteric rendering of Platonism, the line running through Pythagoras, Socrates, Plato, and Plotinus. St. Bonaventura attributed "science" to Aristotelianism and "wisdom" to Platonism.

fit in. As the Intellect is everywhere, its Truth can flash anywhere; but to be steadied, sustained, and increased, a "rheostat" is needed. Traditions are such for the human spirit.

To speak less metaphorically, negatively Schuon doubts that transcendent Truth, the Reality common to the great religions, is directly accessible to many; the mentality of most men and women being exoteric, their choice is between, on the one hand, a faith that is patently exoteric, and on the other, sentimental infatuation with rosy abstractions, this latter resembling being in love with love itself or taking as one's prophet Khalil Gibran. Positively Schuon argues that even esoterics must, almost without exception, submit to exoteric rites. Forms are to be transcended by fathoming their depths and discerning their universal content, not by circumventing them. One might regard them as doorways to be entered, or rather as windows, for the esoteric doesn't leave them behind, but continues to look through them toward the Absolute. But because the symbolism of the spirit always requires that, in the end, space (distance) be transcended, even this will not do. The esoteric finds the Absolute within the traditions as poets find poetry in poems.

3. The Esoteric/Exoteric Distinction Restated

As the esoteric/exoteric distinction is the key to this book, it merits a concluding section devoted to clarifying its character and implications.

Man does not dwell in pure immediacy; he lives in a world of symbolic forms. Transcendence can appear on the human plane only through these forms; it cannot appear directly because it transcends by definition the plane's spatiotemporal categories. Symbols for their part consist of a form/content complex. Exoterics are persons whose meanings derive from forms that are more restricted in scope than are those of esoterics. One is tempted to say that their forms are more concrete, but this could be misleading, for it would imply that esoteric forms are, in contrast, abstract and hence vacuous—shells of reality only, so to speak. Beyond a certain level of generality symbols do appear abstract in this denatured sense to exoterics, but to esoterics they remain full-bodied, if anything thereby gaining in force and reality.

An infant, once he can identify his mother, equates her initially with her tactile or visual presence; if she leaves the room she ceases to exist and the infant cries. Everyone agrees that it is an advance in understanding when "Mother" acquires for the child a reference more extended than "a certain X in my visual or tactile field." But when we continue up the scale of extended meanings to "No man cometh unto the Father, but by me," men divide. For esoterics "me" will designate the Logos. For exoterics, less supple in their capacity for "spiritual abstraction," in precise proportion as the word relaxes its hold on the concrete historical personage of Jesus of Nazareth, the assertion forfeits its saving power.

Another way to indicate the distinction is to say that for the exoteric form and content are less distinguishable. As they present themselves to him as welded together or fused in a homogeneous alloy, he sees no way of having one without the other. By this alternate route we arrive at the same conclusion: forms for exoterics are relatively non-negotiable. Esoterics ride them more loosely, knowing that because they are finite they are, at best, limited keys to the lock, restricted doors to the mystery.

In one of his most powerful analogies, Schuon likens esoterism to command over spiritual space. Anchored to a single spot, the exoteric is unable to circumambulate spiritual objects, so to speak, and this makes it difficult for him to distinguish them as they are in themselves from the way they appear from his frame of reference—a visual example of confounding an idea with the form in which it is clothed. That an idea assumes a form is itself a virtue, for unless it did so it could seldom connect with man. But when a form becomes possessive toward its content, usurping and pre-empting it to itself alone, then instead of opening onto further understandings of the idea through a successive sequence of expanding forms, it runs the danger of becoming paralyzed and constricting.

The tenacity with which the exoteric clings to the forms in which his meanings are manifest is understandable. As he cannot enter concretely into truth on a higher level of universality,* any suggestion to the effect that the forms in which truth comes to him are relative is tantamount to relativism in every sense. Absolutize the relative or fall into relativism—these, for the exoteric, are the only options and he does right of course to choose the former. But his choice is bought at a double price. (1) He will be debarred from according equal rights to other revelations, as the "No man cometh unto the Father" example illustrated. (2) He will encounter theoretical problems that are insuperable—theological instances of Gödel's theorem to the effect that every formal system with precise specifications must contain at least one question that cannot be answered by the stipulations of the system itself. If God is self-sufficient, why did He create the world; if He is perfect, why did He create a world that is imperfect? For exoterism such questions cannot be "brought to heel." For esoterism it is not so much that they have answers as that they do not arise.

The corollaries of the esoteric/exoteric distinction are far-reaching:

For the exoteric, God's personal mode is his only mode; for the esoteric this mode resides in one that is higher and ultimately modeless: the Absolute, the Godhead, Nirguna Brahman of the Vedantists, the Tao that cannot be spoken.

For the exoteric the world is real in every sense; for the esoteric it has only qualified reality from the human standpoint and no separate reality whatsoever from the standpoint of the Godhead. The same holds for the human soul.

For the exoteric, God is primarily loved; for the esoteric He is primarily known; though in the end the exoteric comes to know what he loves and the esoteric to love what he knows.

But this is to point beyond the book in hand to Schuon's work as a whole.

Cambridge, Massachusetts
Summer, 1973

* One must say "universality" rather than "abstraction," for to repeat, though greater universality moves toward abstractness for the exoteric, it moves toward concreteness for the esoteric.

Preface

This book is founded on a doctrine that is metaphysical in the most precise meaning of the word and cannot by any means be described as philosophical. Such a distinction may appear unwarrantable to those who are accustomed to regard metaphysic as a branch of philosophy, but the practice of linking the two together in this manner, although it can be traced back to Aristotle and the Scholastic writers who followed him, merely shows that all philosophy suffers from certain limitations that, even in the most favorable instances such as those just quoted, exclude a completely adequate appreciation of metaphysic. In reality, the transcendent character of metaphysic makes it independent of any purely human mode of thought. In order to define clearly the difference between the two modes in question, it may be said that philosophy proceeds from reason (which is a purely individual faculty), whereas metaphysic proceeds exclusively from the Intellect. The latter faculty has been defined by Meister Eckhart—who fully understood the import of his words—as follows: "There is something in the soul that is uncreate and uncreatable; if the whole soul were this it would be uncreate and uncreatable; and this is the Intellect." An analogous definition, which is still more concise and even richer in symbolic value, is to be found in Moslem esoterism: "The Sufi [that is to say, man identified with the Intellect] is uncreate."

Since purely intellectual knowledge is by definition beyond the reach of the individual, being in its essence supra-individual, universal, or divine, and since it proceeds from pure Intelligence, which is direct and not discursive, it follows that this knowledge not only goes infinitely further than reasoning, but even goes further than faith in the ordinary sense of this term. In other words, intellectual knowledge also transcends the specifically theological point of view, which is itself incomparably superior to the philosophical point of view, since, like metaphysical knowledge, it emanates from God and not from man; but whereas metaphysic proceeds wholly from intellectual intuition, religion proceeds from Revelation. The latter is the Word of God spoken to His creatures, whereas intellectual intuition is a direct and active participation in divine Knowledge and not an indirect and passive participation, as is faith. In other words, in the case of intellectual intuition, knowledge is not possessed by the individual insofar as he is an individual, but insofar as in his innermost essence he is not distinct from his Divine Principle. Thus metaphysical certitude is absolute because of the identity between the knower and the known in the Intellect. If an example may be drawn from the sensory sphere to illustrate the difference between metaphysical and theological knowledge, it may be said that the former, which can be called "esoteric" when it is manifested through a religious symbolism, is conscious of the colorless essence of light and of its character of pure luminosity; a given religious belief, on the other hand, will assert that light is red and not green, whereas another belief will assert the opposite; both will be right insofar as they distinguish light from darkness but not insofar as they identify it with a particular color. This very rudimentary example is designed to show that the theological point of view, because it is based in the minds of believers on a Revelation and not on a knowledge that is accessible to each one of them (an unrealizable condition for a large human collectivity), will of necessity confuse the symbol or form with the naked and supraformal Truth, while metaphysic, which can be compared to a point of view only in a purely provisional sense, will be able to make use of the same symbol or form as a means of expression while at the same time being aware of its relativity. That is why each of the great and intrinsically orthodox religions can, through its dogmas, rites, and other symbols, serve as a means of expression for every truth known directly by the eye of the Intellect, the spiritual organ that is called in Moslem esoterism the "eye of the heart."

We have just stated that religion translates metaphysical or universal truths into dogmatic language. Now, though dogma is not accessible to all men in its intrinsic truth, which can only be directly attained by the Intellect, it is nonetheless accessible through faith, which is, for the great majority, the only possible mode of participation in the Divine Truths. As for intellectual knowledge, which, as we have seen, proceeds neither from belief nor from a process of reasoning, it goes beyond dogma in the sense that, without ever contradicting the latter, it penetrates its internal dimension, that is, the infinite Truth that dominates all forms.

In order to be absolutely clear on this point we must again insist that the rational mode of knowledge in no way extends beyond the realm of generalities and cannot by itself reach any transcendent truth; if it may nevertheless serve as a means of expressing suprarational knowledge—as in the case of Aristotelian and Scholastic ontology—this will always be to the detriment of the intellectual integrity of the doctrine. Some may perhaps object that even the purest metaphysic is sometimes hardly distinguishable from philosophy inasmuch as it uses arguments and seems to reach conclusions. But this resemblance is due merely to the fact that all concepts, once they are expressed, are necessarily clothed in the modes of human thought, which is rational and dialectical. What essentially distinguishes the metaphysical from the philosophical proposition is that the former is symbolical and descriptive, in the sense that it makes use of rational modes as symbols to describe or translate knowledge possessing a greater degree of certainty than any knowledge of a sensible order, whereas philosophy—called, not without reason, *ancilla theologiae*—is never anything more than what it expresses. When philosophy uses reason to resolve a doubt, this proves precisely that its starting point is a doubt that it is striving to overcome, whereas we have seen that the starting point of a metaphysical formulation is always essentially something intellectually evident or certain, which is communicated, to those able to receive it, by symbolical or dialectical means designed to awaken in them the latent knowledge that they bear unconsciously and, it may even be said, eternally within them.

To illustrate the three modes of thought we have been considering, let us apply them to the idea of God. The philosophical point of view, when it does not purely and simply deny God even if only by ascribing to the word a meaning it does not possess, tries to "prove" God by all kinds of argument; in other words, this point of view tries to "prove" either the "existence" or the "non-existence" of God, as though reason, which is only an intermediary and in no wise a source of transcendent knowledge, could "prove" no matter what. Moreover this pretension of reason to autonomy in realms where only intellectual intuition on the one hand and Revelation on the other can communicate knowledge, is characteristic of the philosophical point of view and shows up all its inadequacy. The theological point of view does not, for its part, trouble itself about proving God—it is even prepared to admit that such proof is impossible—but bases itself on belief. It must be added here that "faith" cannot be reduced to a simple matter of belief; otherwise Christ would not have spoken of the "faith which moves mountains," for it goes without saying that ordinary religious belief has no such power. Finally, from the metaphysical standpoint, there is no longer any question either of "proof" or of "belief" but solely of direct evidence, of intellectual evidence that implies absolute certainty; but in the present state of humanity such evidence is only accessible to a spiritual elite that becomes ever more restricted in number. It may be added that religion, by its very nature and independently of any wish of its representatives, who may be unaware of the fact, contains and transmits this purely intellectual Knowledge beneath the veil of its dogmatic and ritual symbols, as we have already seen.

The truths just expressed are not the exclusive possession of any school or individual; were it otherwise they would not be truths, for these cannot be invented, but must necessarily be known in every integral traditional civilization. It might, however, reasonably be asked for what human and cosmic reasons truths that may in a very general sense be called "esoteric" should be brought to light and made explicit at the present time, in an age that is so little inclined to speculation. There is indeed something abnormal in this, but it lies, not in the fact of the exposition of these truths, but in the general conditions of our age, which marks the end of a great cyclic period of terrestrial humanity—the end of a *mahā-yuga* according to Hindu cosmology—and so must recapitulate or manifest again in one way or another everything that is included in the cycle, in conformity with the adage "extremes meet"; thus things that are in themselves abnormal may become necessary by reason of the conditions just referred to. From a more individual point of view, that of mere expediency, it must be admitted that the spiritual confusion of our times has reached such a pitch that the harm that might in principle befall certain people from contact with the truths in question is compensated by the advantages others will derive from the self-same truths; again, the term "esoterism" has been so often misused in order to cloak ideas that are as unspiritual as they are dangerous, and what is known of esoteric doctrines has been so frequently plagiarized and deformed—not to mention the fact that the outward and readily exaggerated incompatibility of the different religious forms greatly discredits, in the minds of most of our contemporaries, all religion—that it is not only desirable but even incumbent upon one to give some idea, firstly, of what true esoterism is and what it is not, and secondly, of what it is that constitutes the profound and eternal solidarity of all spiritual forms.

To come now to the main subject of this book, it must be emphasized that the unity of the different religions is not only unrealizable on the external level, that of the forms themselves, but ought not to be realized at that level, even were this possible, for in that case the revealed forms would be deprived of their sufficient reason. The very fact that they are revealed shows that they are willed by the Divine Word. If the expression "transcendent unity" is used, it means that the unity of the religious forms must be realized in a purely inward and spiritual way and without prejudice to any particular form. The antagonisms between these forms no more affect the one universal Truth than the antagonisms between opposing colors affect the transmission of the one uncolored light (to return to the illustration used already). Just as every color, by its negation of darkness and its affirmation of light, provides the possibility of discovering the ray that makes it visible and of tracing this ray back to its luminous source, so all forms, all symbols, all religions, all dogmas, by their negation of error and their affirmation of Truth, make it possible to follow the ray of Revelation, which is none other than the ray of the Intellect, back to its Divine Source.

THE TRANSCENDENT UNITY OF RELIGIONS

Conceptual Dimensions

The true and complete understanding of an idea goes far beyond the first apprehension of the idea by the intelligence, although more often than not this apprehension is taken for understanding itself. While it is true that the immediate evidence conveyed to us by any particular idea is, on its own level, a real understanding, there can be no question of its embracing the whole extent of the idea, since it is primarily the sign of an aptitude to understand that idea in its completeness. Any truth can in fact be understood at different levels and according to different conceptual dimensions, that is to say, according to an indefinite number of modalities that correspond to all the possible aspects, likewise indefinite in number, of the truth in question. This way of regarding ideas accordingly leads to the question of spiritual realization, the doctrinal expressions of which clearly illustrate the dimensional indefinitude of theoretical conceptions.

Philosophy, considered from the standpoint of its limitations—and it is the limitations of philosophy that confer upon it its specific character—is based on the systematic ignoring of what has been stated above. In other words, philosophy ignores what would be its own negation; moreover, it concerns itself solely with mental schemes that, with its claim to universality, it likes to regard as absolute, although from the point of view of spiritual realization these schemes are merely so many virtual or potential and unused objects, insofar at least as they refer to true ideas; when, however, this is not the case, as practically always occurs in modern philosophy, these schemes are reduced to the condition of mere devices that are unusable from a speculative point of view and are therefore without any real value. As for true ideas, those, that is to say, that more or less implicitly suggest aspects of the total Truth, and hence this Truth itself, they become by that very fact intellectual keys and indeed have no other function; this is something that metaphysical thought alone is capable of grasping. So far as philosophical or ordinary theological thought is concerned, there is, on the contrary, an ignorance affecting not only the nature of the ideas that are believed to be completely understood, but also and above all the scope of theory as such; theoretical understanding is in fact transitory and limited by definition, though its limits can only be more or less approximately defined.

The purely "theoristic" understanding of an idea, which we have so termed because of the limitative tendency that paralyzes it, may justly be characterized by the word "dogmatism"; religious dogma in fact, at least to the extent to which it is supposed to exclude other conceptual forms, though certainly not in itself, represents an idea considered in conformity with a theoristic tendency, and this exclusive way of looking at ideas has even become characteristic of the religious point of view as such. A religious dogma ceases, however, to be limited in this way once it is understood in the light of its inherent truth, which is of a universal order, and this is the case in all esoterism. On the other hand, the ideas formulated in esoterism and in metaphysical doctrines generally may in their turn be understood according to the dogmatic or theoristic tendency, and the case is then analogous to that of the religious dogmatism of which we have just spoken. In this connection, we must again point out that a religious dogma is not a dogma in itself but solely by the fact of being considered as such and through a sort of confusion of the idea with the form in which it is clothed; on the other hand, the outward dogmatization of universal truths is perfectly justified in view of the fact that these truths or ideas, in having to provide the foundation of a religion, must be capable of being assimilated in some degree by all men. Dogmatism as such does not consist in the mere enunciation of an idea, that is to say, in the fact of giving form to a spiritual intuition, but rather in an interpretation that, instead of rejoining the formless and total Truth after taking as its starting point one of the forms of that Truth, results in a sort of paralysis of this form by denying its intellectual potentialities and by attributing to it an absoluteness that only the formless and total Truth itself can possess.

Dogmatism reveals itself not only by its inability to conceive the inward or implicit illimitability of the symbol, the universality that resolves all outward oppositions, but also by its inability to recognize, when faced with two apparently contradictory truths, the inward connection that they implicitly affirm, a connection that makes of them complementary aspects of one and the same truth. One might illustrate this in the following manner: whoever participates in universal Knowledge will regard two apparently contradictory truths as he would two points situated on one and the same circumference that links them together by its continuity and so reduces them to unity; in the measure in which these points are distant from, and thus opposed to, one another, there will be contradiction, and this contradiction will reach its maximum when the two points are situated at the extremities of a diameter of the circle; but this extreme opposition or contradiction only appears as a result of isolating the points under consideration from the circle and ignoring the existence of the latter. One may conclude from this that a dogmatic affirmation, that is to say, an affirmation that is inseparable from its form and admits no other, is comparable to a point, which by definition, as it were, contradicts all other possible points; a speculative formulation, on the other hand, is comparable to an element of a circle, the very form of which indicates its logical and ontological continuity and therefore the whole circle or, by analogical transposition, the whole Truth; this comparison will, perhaps, suggest in the clearest possible way the difference that separates a dogmatic affirmation from a speculative formulation.

The outward and intentional contradictoriness of speculative formulations may show itself, it goes without saying, not only in a single, logically paradoxical formula such as the Vedic *Aham Brahmasmi* ("I am Brahma")—the Vedantic definition of the yogi

—or the *Ana 'l-Ḥaqq* ("I am the Truth") of Al-Ḥallāj, or Christ's words concerning His Divinity, but also, and for even stronger reasons, as between different formulations each of which may be logically homogeneous in itself. Examples of the latter may be found in all sacred Scriptures, notably in the Koran: we need only recall the apparent contradiction between the affirmations regarding predestination and those regarding free will, affirmations that are contradictory only in the sense that they express opposite aspects of a single reality. However, apart from these paradoxical formulations—whether they are so in themselves or in relation to one another—there also remain certain theories that, although expressing the strictest orthodoxy, are nevertheless in outward contradiction one with another, this being due to the diversity of their respective points of view, which are not chosen arbitrarily and artificially but are established spontaneously by virtue of a genuine intellectual originality.

To return to what was said above about the understanding of ideas, a theoretical notion may be compared to the view of an object. Just as this view does not reveal all possible aspects, or in other words, the integral nature of the object, the perfect knowledge of which would be nothing less than identity with it, so a theoretical notion does not itself correspond to the integral truth, of which it necessarily suggests only one aspect, essential or otherwise.* In the example just given error corresponds to an inadequate view of the object whereas a dogmatic conception is comparable

---

* In a treatise directed against rationalist philosophy, Al-Ghazzālī speaks of certain blind men who, not having even a theoretical knowledge of an elephant, came across this animal one day and started to feel the different parts of its body; as a result each man represented the animal to himself according to the part that he touched: for the first, who touched a foot, the elephant resembled a column, whereas for the second, who touched one of the tusks, it resembled a stake, and so on. By this parable Al-Ghazzālī seeks to show the error involved in trying to enclose the universal within a fragmentary notion of it, or within isolated and exclusive aspects or points of view. Shrī Ramakrishna also uses this parable to demonstrate the inadequacy of dogmatic exclusiveness in its negative aspect. The same idea could, however, be expressed by means of an even more adequate example: faced with any object, some might say that it "is" a certain shape, while others might say that it "is" such and such a material; others again might maintain that it "is" such and such a number or such and such a weight, and so forth.

to the exclusive view of one aspect of the object, a view that supposes the immobility of the seeing subject. As for a speculative and therefore intellectually unlimited conception, this may be compared to the sum of all possible views of the object in question, views that presuppose in the subject a power of displacement or an ability to alter his viewpoint, hence a certain mode of identity with the dimensions of space, which themselves effectually reveal the integral nature of the object, at least with respect to its form, which is all that is in question in the example given. Movement in space is in fact an active participation in the possibilities of space, whereas static extension in space, the form of our bodies, for example, is a passive participation in these same possibilities. This may be transposed without difficulty to a higher plane and one may then speak of an "intellectual space," namely, the cognitive all-possibility that is fundamentally the same as the Divine Omniscience, and consequently of "intellectual dimensions" that are the internal modalities of this Omniscience; Knowledge through the Intellect is none other than the perfect participation of the subject in these modalities, and in the physical world this participation is effectually represented by movement. When speaking, therefore, of the understanding of ideas, we may distinguish between a dogmatic understanding, comparable to the view of an object from a single viewpoint, and an integral or speculative understanding, comparable to the indefinite series of possible views of the object, views that are realized through indefinitely multiple changes of point of view. Just as, when the eye changes its position, the different views of an object are connected by a perfect continuity, which represents, so to speak, the determining reality of the object, so the different aspects of a truth, however contradictory they may appear and notwithstanding their indefinite multiplicity, describe the integral Truth that surpasses and determines them. We would again refer here to an illustration we have already used; a dogmatic affirmation corresponds to a point that, as such, contradicts by definition every other point, whereas a speculative formulation is always conceived as an element of a circle that by its very form indicates principially its own continuity, and hence the entire circle and the Truth in its entirety.

It follows from the above that in speculative doctrines it is the point of view on the one hand and the aspect on the other hand that determine the form of the affirmation, whereas in dogmatism the affirmation is confused with a determinate point of view and aspect, thus excluding all others.*

* The Angels are intelligences that are limited to a particular aspect of Divinity; consequently an angelic state is a sort of transcendent point of view. On a lower plane, the "intellectuality" of animals and of the more peripheral species of the terrestrial state, that of plants, for example, corresponds cosmologically to the angelic intellectuality: what differentiates one vegetable species from another is, in reality, simply the mode of its "intelligence"; in other words, it is the form or rather the integral nature of a plant that reveals the state—eminently passive, of course—of contemplation or knowledge of its species; we say "of its species" advisedly, because, considered in isolation, a plant does not constitute an individual. We would recall here that the Intellect, being universal, must be discoverable in everything that exists, to whatever order it belongs; the same is not true of reason, which is only a specifically human faculty and is in no way identical with intelligence, either our own or that of other beings.

The Limitations of Exoterism

1

The exoteric point of view is fundamentally the point of view of individual interest considered in its highest sense, that is to say, extended to cover the whole cycle of existence of the individual and not limited solely to terrestrial life. Exoteric truth is limited by definition, by reason of the very limitation of the end it sets itself, without this restriction, however, affecting the esoteric interpretation of which that same truth is susceptible thanks to the universality of its symbolism, or rather, first and foremost, thanks to the twofold nature, inward and outward, of Revelation itself; whence it follows that a dogma is both a limited idea and an unlimited symbol at one and the same time. To give an example, we may say that the dogma of the unicity of the Church of God must exclude a truth such as that of the validity of other orthodox religious forms, because the idea of religious universality is of no particular usefulness for the purpose of salvation and may even exert a prejudicial effect on it, since, in the case of persons not possessing the capacity to rise above an individual standpoint, this idea would almost inevitably result in religious indifference and hence in the neglect of those religious duties the accomplishment of which is precisely the principal condition of salvation. On the other hand, this same idea of religious universality—an idea that is more or less indispensable to the way of total and disinterested Truth—is nonetheless included symbolically and metaphysically in the dogmatic or theological definition of the Church or of the Mystical Body of Christ; or again, to use the language of the other two monotheistic religions, Judaism and Islam, we may find in the respective conceptions of the "Chosen People," *Yisrā'ēl,* and "submission," *Al-Islām,* a dogmatic symbol of the idea of universal orthodoxy, the *Sanātana Dharma* of the Hindus.

It goes without saying that the outward limitation of dogma, which is precisely what confers upon it its dogmatic character, is perfectly legitimate, since the individual viewpoint to which this limitation corresponds is a reality at its own level of existence. It is because of this relative reality that the individual viewpoint, except to the extent to which it implies the negation of a higher perspective, that is to say, insofar as it is limited by the mere fact of its nature, can and even must be integrated in one fashion or another in every path possessing a transcendent goal. Regarded from this standpoint, exoterism, or rather form as such, will no longer imply an intellectually restricted perspective but will play the part of an accessory spiritual means, without the transcendence of the esoteric doctrine being in any way affected thereby, no limitation being imposed on the latter for reasons of individual expediency. One must not therefore confuse the function of the exoteric viewpoint as such with the function of exoterism as a spiritual means: the viewpoint in question is incompatible, in one and the same consciousness, with esoteric knowledge, for the latter dissolves this viewpoint as a preliminary to reabsorbing it into the center from which it came; but the exoteric means do not for that reason cease to be utilizable, and will, in fact, be used in two ways: on the one hand, by intellectual transposition into the esoteric order—in which case they will act as supports of intellectual actualization; and on the other hand, by their regulating action on the individual portion of the being.

The exoteric aspect of a religion is thus a providential disposition that, far from being blameworthy, is necessary in view of the fact that the esoteric way can only concern a minority, especially under the present conditions of terrestrial humanity. What is blameworthy is not the existence of exoterism, but rather its all-invading autocracy—due primarily perhaps, in the Christian world, to the narrow precision of the Latin mind—which causes many of those who would be qualified for the way of pure Knowledge not only to stop short at the outward aspect of the religion, but even to reject entirely an esoterism that they know only through a veil of prejudice and deformation, unless indeed, not finding anything in exoterism to satisfy their intelligence, they be caused to stray into false and artificial doctrines in an attempt to find something that exoterism does not offer them, and even takes it upon itself to prohibit.*

The exoteric viewpoint is, in fact, doomed to end by negating itself once it is no longer vivified by the presence within it of the esoterism of which it is both the outward radiation and the veil. So it is that religion, according to the measure in which it denies metaphysical and initiatory realities and becomes crystallized in a literalistic dogmatism, inevitably engenders unbelief; the atrophy that overtakes dogmas when they are deprived of their internal dimension recoils upon them from the outside, in the form of heretical and atheistic negations.

2

The presence of an esoteric nucleus in a civilization that is specifically exoteric in character guarantees to it a normal development and a maximum of stability; this nucleus, however, is not in any sense a part, even an inner part, of the exoterism, but represents, on the contrary, a quasi-independent "dimension" in relation to the latter.† Once this dimension or nucleus ceases to exist, which

* This recalls the denunciation uttered by Christ: "Woe unto you, lawyers! for ye have taken away the key of knowledge: ye entered not in yourselves, and them that were entering in, ye hindered" (Luke xi. 52).

† So far as the Islamic religion is concerned, we may quote the following observations of an Indian Moslem prince: "The majority of non-Moslems, and even many Moslems who have been brought up in a European cultural environment, are ignorant of this particular element of Islam which is both its marrow and its centre, which gives life and force to its outer forms and activities and which by reason of the universal nature of its content can call to witness the disciples of other religions" (Nawab A. Hydari Hydar Nawaz Jung Bahadur, in his preface to *Studies in Tasawwuf* by Khaja Khan).

can only happen in quite abnormal, though cosmologically necessary, circumstances, the religious edifice is shaken, or even suffers a partial collapse, and finally becomes reduced to its most external elements, namely, literalism and sentimentality.* Moreover, the most tangible criteria of such a decadence are, on the one hand, the failure to recognize, even to the point of denial, metaphysical and initiatory exegesis, that is to say, the mystical sense of the Scriptures —an exegesis that has moreover a close connection with all aspects of the intellectuality of the religious form under consideration; and on the other hand, the rejection of sacred art, that is to say, of the inspired and symbolic forms by means of which that intellectuality is radiated and so communicated in an immediate and unrestricted language to all intelligences. This may not perhaps be quite sufficient to explain why it is that exoterism has indirectly need of esoterism, we do not say in order to enable it to exist, since the mere fact of its existence is not in question any more than the incorruptibility of its means of grace, but simply to enable it to exist in normal conditions. The fact is that the presence of this transcendent dimension at the center of the religious form provides its exoteric side with a life-giving sap, universal and Paracletic in its essence, without which it will be compelled to fall back entirely upon itself and, thus left to its own resources, which are limited by definition, will end by becoming a sort of massive and opaque body the very density of which will inevitably produce fissures, as is shown by the modern history of Christianity. In other words, when exoterism is deprived of the complex and subtle interferences of its transcendent dimension, it finds itself ultimately overwhelmed by the exteriorized consequences of its own limitations, the latter having become, as it were, total.

Now, if one proceeds from the idea that exoterists do not understand esoterism and that they have in fact a right not to understand it or even to consider it nonexistent, one must also

---

* Hence the increasingly marked predominance of "literature," in the derogatory sense of the word, over genuine intellectuality on the one hand and true piety on the other; hence also the exaggerated importance accorded to more or less futile activities of every kind that always carefully avoid the "one thing necessary."

recognize their right to condemn certain manifestations of esoterism that seem to encroach on their own territory and cause "offence," to use the Gospel expression; but how is one to explain the fact that in most, if not all, cases of this nature, the accusers divest themselves of this right by the iniquitous manner in which they proceed? It is certainly not their more or less natural incomprehension, nor the defense of their genuine right, but solely the perfidiousness of the means that they employ that constitutes what amounts to a "sin against the Holy Ghost";* this perfidiousness proves, moreover, that the accusations that they find it necessary to formulate, generally serve only as a pretext for gratifying an instinctive hatred of everything that seems to threaten their superficial equilibrium, which is really only a form of individualism, therefore of ignorance.

3

We remember once hearing it said that "metaphysic is not necessary for salvation"; now this is basically false as a generalization, since a man who is a metaphysician by nature and is aware of it cannot find his salvation by the negation of the very thing that draws him toward God; moreover, any spiritual life must of necessity be based on a natural predisposition that determines its mode,

---

* Thus neither lack of understanding on the part of the religious authority concerned, nor even a certain basis of truth in the accusations brought by it, can excuse the iniquity of the proceedings instituted against the Sufi Al-Hallāj, any more than the incomprehension of the Jews can excuse the iniquity of their proceedings against Christ.

In a similar connection, one may ask why so much stupidity and bad faith are to be found in religious polemics, even among men who are otherwise free from such failings; this is a sure sign that the majority of these polemics are tainted with the "sin against the Holy Ghost." No blame can be attached to a person for attacking a foreign religion in the name of his own belief, if it is done purely and simply through ignorance; when, however, this is not the case, the person will be guilty of blasphemy, since, by outraging the Divine Truth in an alien form, he is merely profiting by an opportunity to offend God without having to trouble his own conscience. This is the real explanation of the gross and impure zeal displayed by those who, in the name of their religious convictions, devote their lives to making sacred things appear odious, a task they can only accomplish by contemptible methods.

and this is what is termed "vocation"; no spiritual authority would advise a man to follow a way for which he was not made. This is the lesson of the parable of the talents, to mention but one example, and the same meaning is implicit in the following texts from St. James: "For whosoever shall keep the whole law and yet offend in one point, he is guilty of all," and "therefore, to him that knoweth to do good and doeth it not, to him is sin"; now the essence of the Law, according to Christ's words, is to love God with our whole being, including the intelligence that is its central part. In other words, since we should love God with all that we are, we should also love Him with our intelligence, which is the best part of us. No one will contest the fact that intelligence is not a feeling but something infinitely greater; it follows, therefore, that the word "love" as used in the New Testament to indicate the relationship that exists between man and God, and especially between God and man, cannot be understood in a purely sentimental sense and must mean something more than mere desire. On the other hand, if love is the inclining of one being toward another, with a view to union, it is Knowledge that, by definition, will bring about the most perfect union between man and God, since it alone appeals to what is already divine in man, namely the Intellect; this supreme mode of the love of God is therefore by far the highest human possibility and no man can wilfully ignore it without "sinning against the Holy Ghost." To pretend that metaphysic, in itself and for all men, is a superfluous thing and in no case necessary for salvation, amounts not only to misjudging its nature, but also to denying the right to exist to those men who have been endowed by God with the quality of intelligence in a transcendent degree.

A further observation should also be made that is relevant to this question. Salvation is merited by action, in the widest sense of the word, and this explains why certain people can be led into disparaging intelligence, since the latter may render action superfluous, while its wider possibilities show up the relativity of merit and of the perspective attached to it. Also the specifically religious point of view has a tendency to consider pure intellectuality, which it hardly ever distinguishes from mere rationality, as being more or less opposed to meritorious action and therefore dangerous for salvation; it is for this reason that there are people who are quite ready to attribute to intelligence a luciferian aspect and who speak without hesitation of "intellectual pride," as if this were not a contradiction in terms; hence also the exaltation of "childlike" or "simple" faith, which indeed we are the first to respect when it is spontaneous and natural, but not when it is theoretical and affected.

It is not uncommon to hear the following view expressed: since salvation implies a state of perfect beatitude and religion insists upon nothing more, why choose the way that has "deification" for its goal? To this objection we will reply that the esoteric way, by definition, cannot be the object of a choice by those who follow it, for it is not the man who chooses the way, it is the way that chooses the man. In other words, the question of a choice does not arise, since the finite cannot choose the Infinite; rather the question is one of vocation, and those who are "called," to use the Gospel expression, cannot ignore the call without committing a "sin against the Holy Ghost," any more than a man can legitimately ignore the obligations of his religion.

If it is incorrect to speak of a "choice" with reference to the Infinite, it is equally wrong to speak of a "desire," since it is less a desire for Divine Reality that characterizes the initiate than a logical and ontological tendency toward his own transcendent Essence. This definition is of extreme importance.

4

Exoteric doctrine as such, considered, that is to say, apart from the "spiritual influence" that is capable of acting on souls independently of it, by no means possesses absolute certitude. Theological knowledge cannot by itself shut out the temptations of doubt, even in the case of great mystics; as for the influences of Grace that may intervene in such cases, they are not consubstantial with the intelligence, so that their permanence does not depend on the being who benefits from them. Exoteric ideology being limited to a relative point of view, that of individual salvation—an interested point of view that even influences the conception of Divinity in a restrictive sense—possesses no means of proof or doctrinal credentials proportionate to its own exigencies. Every exoteric doctrine is in fact characterized by a disproportion between its dogmatic demands and its dialectical guarantees: for its demands are absolute as deriving from the Divine Will and therefore also from Divine Knowledge, whereas its guarantees are relative, because they are independent of this Will and based, not on Divine Knowledge, but on a human point of view, that of reason and sentiment. For instance, Brahmins are invited to abandon completely a religion that has lasted for several thousands of years, one that has provided the spiritual support of innumerable generations and has produced flowers of wisdom and holiness down to our times. The arguments that are produced to justify this extraordinary demand are in no wise logically conclusive, nor do they bear any proportion to the magnitude of the demand; the reasons that the Brahmins have for remaining faithful to their spiritual patrimony are therefore infinitely stronger than the reasons by which it is sought to persuade them to cease being what they are. The disproportion, from the Hindu point of view, between the immense reality of the Brahmanic tradition and the insufficiency of the religious counter-arguments is such as to prove quite sufficiently that had God wished to submit the world to one religion only, the arguments put forward on behalf of this religion would not be so feeble, nor those of certain so-called "infidels" so powerful; in other words, if God were on the side of one religious form only, the persuasive power of this form would be such that no man of good faith would be able to resist it. Moreover, the application of the term "infidel" to civilizations that are, with one exception, very much older than Christianity and that have every spiritual and historic right to ignore the latter, provides a further demonstration, by the very illogicality of its naïve pretensions, of the perverted nature of the religious claims with regard to other orthodox traditional forms.

An absolute requirement to believe in one particular religion and not in another cannot in fact be justified save by eminently relative means, as, for example, by attempted philosophico-theological, historical, or sentimental proofs; in reality, however, no proofs exist in support of such claims to the unique and exclusive truth, and any attempt so made can only concern the individual dispositions of men, which, being ultimately reducible to a question of credulity, are as relative as can be. Every exoteric perspective claims, by definition, to be the only true and legitimate one. This is because the exoteric point of view, being concerned only with an individual interest, namely, salvation, has no advantage to gain from knowledge of the truth of other religious forms. Being uninterested as to its own deepest truth, it is even less interested in the truth of other religions, or rather it denies this truth, since the idea of a plurality of religious forms might be prejudicial to the exclusive pursuit of individual salvation. This clearly shows up the relativity of form as such, though the latter is nonetheless an absolute necessity for the salvation of the individual. It might be asked, however, why the guarantees, that is to say, the proofs of veracity or credibility, which religious polemists do their utmost to produce, do not derive spontaneously from the Divine Will, as is the case with religious demands. Obviously such a question has no meaning unless it relates to truths, for one cannot prove errors; the arguments of religious controversy are, however, in no way related to the intrinsic and positive domain of faith; an idea that has only an extrinsic and negative significance and that, fundamentally, is merely the result of an induction—such, for example, as the idea of the exclusive truth and legitimacy of a particular religion or, which comes to the same thing, of the falsity and illegitimacy of all other possible religions—an idea such as this evidently cannot be the object of proof, whether this proof be divine or, for still stronger reasons, human. So far as genuine dogmas are concerned —that is to say, dogmas that are not derived by induction but are of a strictly intrinsic character—if God has not given theoretical proofs of their truth it is, in the first place, because such proofs are inconceivable and nonexistent on the exoteric plane, and to demand them as unbelievers do would be a pure and simple contradiction; secondly, as we shall see later, if such proofs do in fact exist, it is on quite a different plane, and the Divine Revelation most certainly implies them, without any omission. Moreover, to return to the exoteric plane where alone this question is relevant, the Revelation in its essential aspect is sufficiently intelligible to enable it to serve as a vehicle for the action of Grace,* and Grace is the only sufficient and fully valid reason for adhering to a religion. However, since this action of Grace only concerns those who do not in fact possess its equivalent under some other revealed form, the dogmas remain without persuasive power—we may say without proofs—for those who do possess this equivalent. Such people are therefore "unconvertible"—leaving aside certain cases of conversion due to the suggestive force of a collective psychism, in which case Grace intervenes only *a posteriori*,† for the spiritual influence can have no hold over them, just as one light cannot illuminate another. This is in conformity with the Divine Will, which has distributed the one Truth under different forms or, to express it in another way, between different humanities, each one of which is symbolically the only one. It may be added that if the extrinsic relativity of exoterism is in conformity with the Divine Will, which affirms itself in this way according to the very nature of things, it goes without saying that this relativity cannot be done away with by any human will.

Thus, having shown that no rigorous proof exists to support an exoteric claim to the exclusive possession of the truth, must we not

* A typical example of conversion by spiritual influence or Grace, without any doctrinal argument, is afforded by the well-known case of Sundar Singh; this Sikh, who was of noble birth and the possessor of a mystical temperament, though lacking in real intellectual qualities, was the sworn enemy, not only of Christians, but of Christianity and Christ Himself; his hatred, by reason of its paradoxical coexistence with his noble and mystical nature, came up against the spiritual influence of Christ and turned to despair; then he had a vision that brought about an immediate conversion. The interesting point is that Christian doctrine took no part in his conversion and the idea of seeking religious orthodoxy had never even occurred to him. The case of St. Paul presents certain purely technical analogies with this example, though on a considerably higher level as regards both the person involved and the circumstances. As a general proposition it can be stated that when a man possessing a religious nature hates and persecutes a religion, he is, circumstances permitting, on the verge of being converted to it.

† This applies to those non-Christians who become converted to Christianity in much the same way that they adopt no matter what form of modern Western civilization. The thirst for novelty characteristic of the West is replaced in the case of these converts by a thirst for change, or one might say for denial; in both cases we find the same tendency to realize and exhaust possibilities that the traditional civilization had excluded.

now go further and admit that even the orthodoxy of a religious form cannot be proved? Such a conclusion would be highly artificial and, in any case, completely erroneous, since there is implicit in every religious form an absolute proof of its truth and so of its orthodoxy; what cannot be proved, for want of absolute proof, is not the intrinsic truth, hence the traditional legitimacy, of a form of the universal Revelation, but solely the hypothetical fact that any particular form is the only true and legitimate one, and if this cannot be proved it is for the simple reason that it is untrue.

There are, therefore, irrefutable proofs of the truth of a religion; but these proofs, which are of a purely spiritual order, while being the only possible proofs in support of a revealed truth, entail at the same time a denial of the pretensions to exclusiveness of the form. In other words, he who sets out to prove the truth of one religion either has no proofs, since such proofs do not exist, or else he has the proofs that affirm all religious truth without exception, whatever the form in which it may have clothed itself.

5

The exoteric claim to the exclusive possession of a unique truth, or of Truth without epithet, is therefore an error purely and simply; in reality, every expressed truth necessarily assumes a form, that of its expression, and it is metaphysically impossible that any form should possess a unique value to the exclusion of other forms; for a form, by definition, cannot be unique and exclusive, that is to say, it cannot be the only possible expression of what it expresses. Form implies specification or distinction, and the specific is only conceivable as a modality of a "species," that is to say, of a category that includes a combination of analogous modalities. Again, that which is limited excludes by definition whatever is not comprised within its own limits and must compensate for this exclusion by a reaffirmation or repetition of itself outside its own boundaries, which amounts to saying that the existence of other limited things is rigorously implied in the very definition of the limited. To claim that a limitation, for example, a form considered as such, is unique and incomparable of its kind, and that it excludes the existence of other analogous modalities, is to attribute to it the unicity of Existence itself; now, no one can contest the fact that a form is always a limitation or that a religion is of necessity always a form—not, that goes without saying, by virtue of its internal Truth, which is of a universal and supraformal order, but because of its mode of expression, which, as such, cannot but be formal and therefore specific and limited. It can never be said too often that a form is always a modality of a category of formal, and therefore distinctive or multiple, manifestation, and is consequently but one modality among others that are equally possible, their supraformal cause alone being unique. We will also repeat—for this is metaphysically of great importance—that a form, by the very fact that it is limited, necessarily leaves something outside itself, namely, that which its limits exclude; and this something, if it belongs to the same order, is necessarily analogous to the form under consideration, since the distinction between forms must needs be compensated by an indistinction or relative identity that prevents them from being absolutely distinct from each other, for that would entail the absurd idea of a plurality of unicities or Existences, each form representing a sort of divinity without any relationship to other forms.

As we have just seen, the exoteric claim to the exclusive possession of the truth comes up against the axiomatic objection that there is no such thing in existence as a unique fact, for the simple reason that it is strictly impossible that such a fact should exist, unicity alone being unique and no fact being unicity; it is this that is ignored by the ideology of the "believers," which is fundamentally nothing but an intentional and interested confusion between the formal and the universal. The ideas that are affirmed in one religious form (as, for example, the idea of the Word or of the Divine Unity) cannot fail to be affirmed, in one way or another, in all other religious forms; similarly the means of grace or of spiritual realization at the disposal of one priestly order cannot but possess their equivalent elsewhere; and indeed, the more important and indispensable any particular means of grace may be, the more certain is it that it will be found in all the orthodox forms in a mode appropriate to the environment in question.

The foregoing can be summed up in the following formula: pure and absolute Truth can only be found beyond all its possible expressions; these expressions, as such, cannot claim the attributes of this Truth; their relative remoteness from it is expressed by their differentiation and multiplicity, by which they are strictly limited.

6

The metaphysical impossibility of the exclusive possession of the truth by any doctrinal form whatsoever can also be expressed in the following manner, adopting a cosmological viewpoint that can be translated without difficulty into religious language. That God should have permitted the decay and consequent decline of certain civilizations after having granted them several thousand years of spiritual prosperity is in no way in contradiction with the nature of God, if one may so express oneself. Likewise, that the whole of humanity should have entered into a relatively short period of obscuration after thousands of years of sane and balanced existence is again in conformity with God's manner of acting. On the other hand, to suppose that God, while desiring the well-being of humanity, should have seen fit to leave the vast majority of men —including the most gifted—to stagnate for thousands of years, practically without hope, in the darkness of mortal ignorance, and that in wishing to save the human race He should have seen fit to choose a means so materially and psychologically ineffective as a new religion that, long before it could be brought to the notice of all mankind, had not only acquired an increasingly particularized and local character, but was even, by force of circumstances, partially corrupted in its original environment—to suppose that God could act in such a manner is highly presumptuous and flagrantly contradicts the nature of God, the essence of which is Goodness and Mercy. This nature, as theology is far from being unaware, can be "terrible" but not monstrous. Again, that God should have allowed human blindness to create heresies within traditional civilizations is in conformity with the Divine Laws that govern the whole of creation; but that God could have allowed a religion that was merely the invention of a man to conquer a part of humanity and to maintain itself for more than a thousand years in a quarter of the inhabited world, thus betraying the love, faith, and hope of a multitude of sincere and fervent souls—this again is contrary to the Laws of the Divine Mercy, or in other words, to those of Universal Possibility.

The Redemption is an eternal act that cannot be situated in either time or space, and the sacrifice of Christ is a particular manifestation or realization of it on the human plane; men were able to benefit from the Redemption as well before the coming of Jesus Christ as after it, and outside the visible Church as well as within it.

If Christ had been the only manifestation of the Word, supposing such a uniqueness of manifestation to be possible, the effect of His birth would have been the instantaneous reduction of the universe to ashes.

7

We have seen above that everything that can be said concerning dogmas applies equally to means of Grace, such as the sacraments. Thus, if it be true that the Eucharist is a means of grace of primordial importance, this is because it emanates from a universal Reality from which it draws all its own reality; but if this be so, the Eucharist, like all other corresponding means of Grace in other religious forms, cannot be unique, since a universal Reality cannot have only one manifestation to the exclusion of any others, for in that case it would not be universal. It is no use objecting that this rite concerns the whole of humanity, on the ground that it must be taken to "all nations," to use the Gospel expression; for the world in its normal state, at least since the beginning of a particular cyclic period, is composed of several distinct humanities who are more or less ignorant of each other's existence, though in certain respects and under certain circumstances the exact delimitation of these humanities may be a highly complex question owing to the intervention of exceptional cyclic conditions.*

Though it is true that some of the great Prophets or *Avatāras,* while being aware, in principle, of the universality of religion, have been impelled to deny certain religious forms in a purely outward sense, it is necessary to consider, firstly, the immediate reason for this attitude, and secondly, its symbolic meaning, the latter being superimposed, so to speak, on the former. If Abraham, Moses, and Christ denied the "paganisms" with which they came into contact, the reason is that they were dealing with religions that had outlived their usefulness; surviving as mere forms without any true spiritual life and sometimes even serving as supports for sinister influences, the reason for their existence had disappeared. One who is "chosen" and who is himself the living tabernacle of the Truth certainly has no cause to respect dead forms that have become unfitted to fulfill their original purpose. On the other hand, this negative attitude on the part of those who manifest the Divine Word is also symbolic, and it is that which gives to it its deepest and truest meaning; for while it clearly could not concern such kernels of esoterism as may have survived in the midst of civilizations that were outworn and had been emptied of their meaning, this same attitude is, on the contrary, fully justified when applied to a state of fact, that is to say, to a degeneracy or "paganism" that had become widespread. To give another analogous example: if Islam had in some measure to deny the monotheistic forms that preceded it, the immediate reason lay in the formal limitations of those religions. It is, for instance, beyond doubt that

---

* Certain passages from the New Testament indicate that for the Christian religion the "world" is identified with the Roman Empire, which represented the providential sphere of expansion and life for Christian civilization. Thus St. Luke wrote—or rather the Holy Ghost made St. Luke write—that "in those days there went out a decree from Caesar Augustus that all the world should be taxed" (ἀπογράφεσθαι πᾶσαν τὴν οἰκουμένην, *ut describeretur universus orbis*), to which Dante made allusion in his treatise on the monarchy when he spoke of the "census of the human race" (*in illa singulari generis humani descriptione*). Elsewhere in the same treatise we find the following: "By these words, we may clearly understand that universal jurisdiction over the world belonged to the Romans," and also: "I therefore affirm that the Roman people . . . has acquired . . . dominion over all mortals."

Judaism was no longer capable of serving as a religious basis for the peoples of the Near East, since the Judaic form had become too particularized to be suitable for expansion; as for Christianity, not only had it very soon become particularized in a similar way, under the influence of its Western environment and perhaps more especially of the Roman mind, but it had also given birth in Arabia and the adjacent countries to all manner of deviations that threatened to inundate the Near East, and even India, with a multitude of heresies that were far removed from primitive and orthodox Christianity. The Islamic Revelation, by virtue of the Divine authority inherent in every Revelation, clearly had the most indisputable right to reject the Christian dogmas, which, moreover, were all the more liable to give rise to deviations in that they were initiatory truths that had been popularized rather than genuinely adapted. On the other hand, the passages in the Koran concerning Christians, Jews, Sabaeans, and pagans have primarily a symbolic meaning that has no bearing on the orthodoxy of the religions, and their mention by name is simply a means of describing certain conditions affecting humanity in general. For instance, when it is stated in the Koran that Abraham was neither Jew nor Christian but *hanīf* ("orthodox" in relation to the Primordial Tradition), it is clear that the names "Jew" and "Christian" can only be intended to denote certain general spiritual attitudes of which the formal limitations of Judaism and Christianity are but particular manifestations or examples. In speaking of the formal limitations of Judaism and Christianity we are not of course referring to Judaism and Christianity in themselves, their orthodoxy not being in dispute.

Returning to the question of the relative incompatibility between the different religious forms and more particularly between certain of them, we may add that it is necessary that one form should to some extent misinterpret the others, since the reason for the existence of a religion, from one point of view at least, is to be found precisely in those things wherein it differs from other religions. Divine Providence has permitted no mingling of the revealed forms since the time when humanity became divided into different "humanities" and moved away from the Primordial Tradition, the only unique religion possible. For example, the Moslem misinterpretation of the Christian dogma of the Trinity is providential, since the doctrine contained in this dogma is essentially and exclusively esoteric and is not capable of being "exotericized" in any way whatever; Islam had therefore to limit the expansion of this dogma, but this in no way prejudices the existence, within Islam, of the universal truth that is expressed by the dogma in question. On the other hand, it may be useful to point out here that the deification of Jesus and Mary, indirectly attributed to the Christians by the Koran, gives rise to a "Trinity" that this Book nowhere identifies with the Trinity of Christian doctrine but that is nonetheless based on certain realities: firstly, the idea of the "Co-Redemptress," "Mother of God," a nonexoteric doctrine that as such could find no place in the religious perspective of Islam; secondly, the Marianism that existed in practice and that from the Islamic point of view constituted a partial usurpation of the worship due to God; and lastly, the "Mariolatry" of certain Oriental sects against which Islam was bound to react all the more violently in that it bore a close resemblance to Arab paganism. On the other hand, according to the Sufi 'Abd al-Karīm al-Jīlī, the "Trinity" mentioned in the Koran is capable of an esoteric interpretation—the Gnostics in fact looked upon the Holy Ghost as the "Divine Mother"—and it is accordingly only for the exteriorization or alteration of this meaning, as the case may be, that orthodox Christians and the heretical worshippers of the Virgin are respectively reproached. From yet another viewpoint it may be said—and the very existence of the heretics in question proves it—that the Koranic "Trinity" corresponds fundamentally to what the Christian dogmas would have become through an inevitable fault of adaptation had they come to be adopted by the Arabs, for whom they were not intended. So far as the orthodox Christian interpretation of the dogma of the Trinity is concerned, its rejection by Islam is also motivated by considerations of a purely metaphysical kind. Christian theology understands by the Holy Ghost not only a purely principial Reality, metacosmic and Divine, but also the direct reflection of this Reality in the manifested, cosmic, and created order; according to the theological definition, in fact, the Holy Ghost, apart from its principial or Divine signification, embraces also the summit or luminous center of the whole creation, that is to say, it embraces supraformal manifestation, which, to use Hindu terms, is the direct and central reflection of the creative Principle, *Purusha,* in the cosmic Substance, *Prakriti*. This reflection, which is the Divine Intelligence manifested, or *Buddhi*—in Sufism *Ar-Rūḥ* and *Al-'Aql,* and also the four Archangels who are analogous to the Devas and their Shaktis and represent so many aspects or functions of this Intelligence—is the Holy Ghost insofar as It illumines, inspires, and sanctifies man. When theology identifies this reflection with God, it is right in the sense that *Buddhi* or *Ar-Rūḥ*—the Metatron of the Kabbalah—"is" God in the essential or "vertical" relationship, namely, in the sense that a reflection is "essentially" identical with its cause. When, on the other hand, the same theology distinguishes the Archangels from God the Holy Ghost, and regards them solely as creatures, it is again right, since it then distinguishes the Holy Ghost reflected in creation from Its principial and Divine prototype. It is, however, inconsistent, and necessarily so, in failing to take into account the fact that the Archangels are aspects or functions of this central or supreme portion of the creation that is the Holy Ghost qua Paraclete. From a theological or exoteric point of view, it is not possible to admit, on the one hand, the difference between the Divine, principial, metacosmic Holy Ghost and the manifested, cosmic, and therefore created Holy Ghost, and on the other hand, the identity of the latter with the Archangels. The theological point of view, in fact, can never combine two different perspectives in a single dogma and this accounts for the divergence between Christianity and Islam: for the latter, the Christian deification of the cosmic Intellect constitutes an "association" *(shirk)* of something created—though it be the formless, angelic, paradisiacal, or Paracletic manifestation—with God. This question of the Holy Ghost apart, Islam would in no way oppose the idea that Divine Unity comprises a ternary aspect; what it rejects is solely the idea that God is exclusively and absolutely a Trinity, since from an Islamic point of view, this amounts to ascribing relativity to God, or to attributing to Him a relative aspect in an absolute sense.

When we say that a religious form is made, if not for a particular race, at least for a human collectivity determined by certain particular conditions—conditions that may be of a highly complex nature, as in the case of the Islamic world—the fact that Christians are to be found among practically all peoples or any other similar argument cannot be raised as a valid objection. In order to appreciate the necessity for a religious form, it is not relevant to know whether or not, within the collectivity for which this form was made, there exist some individuals or groups capable of adapting themselves to another form—this could not be disputed —but solely whether the whole collectivity could adapt itself to the form in question; for instance, for the purpose of putting the legitimacy of Islam in doubt, it is not sufficient merely to point out that there are some Arab Christians, since the only question to consider is what kind of a Christianity would emerge if it came to be professed by the whole Arab collectivity.

There should now be no difficulty in understanding that the Divinity manifests Its Personal aspect through each particular Revelation and Its supreme Impersonality through the diversity of the forms of Its Word.

8

It was pointed out earlier that in its normal state humanity is composed of several distinct "worlds." Certain people will doubtless object that Christ, when speaking of the "world," never suggested any such delimitation, and furthermore that He made no reference to the existence of an esoterism. To this it may be answered that neither did He explain to the Jews how they should interpret those of His words that scandalized them. Moreover, an esoterism is addressed precisely to those "that have ears to hear" and who for that reason have no need of the explanations and "proofs" that may be desired by those for whom esoterism is not intended. As for the teaching that Christ may have reserved for His disciples, or some of them, it did not have to be set forth explicitly in the Gospels, since it is contained therein in a synthetic and symbolic form, the only form admitted in sacred Scriptures.

Futhermore, as a Divine Incarnation, Christ necessarily spoke from an absolute standpoint, by reason of a certain "subjectivization" of the Absolute that takes place in the case of "God-men," concerning which, however, we cannot speak at length here.* He therefore had no occasion to take account of contingencies outside the sphere of His mission, nor did He have to specify the existence of traditional worlds that were "whole"—to use the Gospel term—lying outside the "sick" world with which His message was concerned; nor was He called upon to explain that in naming Himself "the Way, the Truth, and the Life"† in an absolute or principial sense He was not thereby trying to limit the universal manifestation of the Word, but was on the contrary affirming His own essential identity with the Word, the cosmic manifestation of which He Himself was living in subjective mode. This shows the impossibility of such a being considering Himself from the ordinary point of view of relative existence, although this point of view is included in every human nature and must be affirmed incidentally; but this in no way concerns the specifically exoteric perspective.

To return to the questions we were considering earlier, it must be added that since the expansion of the West over the rest of the world, exoteric incomprehension has ceased to be a matter of indifference, since it may compromise the Christian religion itself in

---

* René Guénon explains this "subjectivization" in the following terms:

The lives of certain beings, considered from the standpoint of individual appearances, contain occurrences that correspond with events taking place in the cosmic order and outwardly may be said to represent an image or a reproduction of the latter; but from an inward standpoint this relationship must be reversed, for, since these beings are really the *Mahā-Purusha,* the cosmic events are truly speaking modelled on their lives, or to be more exact, on the reality of which these lives are a direct expression, the cosmic events themselves being only a reflected expression of this reality. [*Études Traditionnelles,* March, 1939]

† In Sufism there is a saying that "None may meet Allāh who has not first met the Prophet"; that is to say, none can attain God save by means of His Word, in whatever form the latter may be revealed; or again, in a more specifically initiatory sense: None can attain the Divine Self except through the perfection of the human ego. It is important to emphasize that when Christ says, "I am the Way, the Truth, and the Life," this is absolutely true of the Divine Word ("Christ"), and relatively true of its human manifestation ("Jesus"); an absolute truth cannot in fact be limited to a relative being. Jesus is God, but God is not Jesus; Christianity is Divine, but God is not Christian.

the eyes of those who begin to perceive that not everything outside this religion is dark paganism. Needless to say, there is no question of reproaching Christ's teaching with any omission, since He was speaking to His Church and not to the modern world, which, as such, owes its whole existence to its rupture with this Church and therefore to its infidelity toward Christ. However, the Gospels do in fact contain some allusions to the limits of the Christian mission and to the existence of religious worlds that are not identifiable with paganism: "They that be whole need not a physician, but they that are sick"; and again: "For I am not come to call the righteous, but sinners to repentance" (Matt. 9:12, 13); and finally this verse, which clearly explains the nature of paganism: "Therefore take no thought, saying: What shall we eat? or, What shall we drink? or, Wherewithal shall we be clothed? For after all these things do the Gentiles [pagans] seek" (Matt. 6:31, 32).* It is also possible to quote the following passages in a similar sense: "Verily I say unto you, I have not found so great faith, no, not in Israel. And I say unto you that many shall come from the East and West and shall sit at the feast† with Abraham and Isaac and Jacob, in the Kingdom of Heaven. But the children of the kingdom [Israel, the Church] shall be cast out into outer darkness" (Matt. 8:10–12), and: "For he that is not against us is on our part" (Mark 9:40).

We have stated that Christ, in His capacity as a Divine Incarnation and in conformity with the universal essence of His teaching, always spoke from an absolute standpoint, that is to say, He symbolically identified certain facts with the principles that they translate, without ever placing Himself at the point of view of those for

---

* In fact, the ancient paganism, including that of the Arabs, was distinguished by its practical materialism, whereas it is impossible in good faith to make the same reproach against the Oriental religions that have maintained themselves up to our day.

† This example of Oriental symbolism, or of symbolism without further qualification, should be sufficient to show the prejudice of those who decry the Islamic Paradise. Moreover, the "fire" of hell, which Christians admit no less than Moslems do, is logically just as "sensuous" as the "feast" or the "houris."

whom the facts presented an interest in themselves.* Such an attitude may be illustrated in the following way: would anyone speaking of the sun seriously contend that the placing of the definite article before the word "sun" was tantamount to denying the existence of other suns in space? What makes it possible to speak of the sun, without specifying that it refers to one sun among others, is precisely the fact that for our world the sun we know is truly "*the* sun," and it is solely in this capacity, and not insofar as it is one sun among others, that it reflects the Divine Unicity. The sufficient reason for a Divine Incarnation is the quality of unicity that it derives from That which it incarnates, and not the quality of fact that it necessarily derives from manifestation.†

* In the language of Christ, the destruction of Jerusalem is symbolically identified with the Last Judgment, which is very characteristic of the God-man's synthetic and, so to speak, essential or absolute manner of viewing things. The same remark applies with regard to his prophecies concerning the descent of the Holy Ghost: they embrace simultaneously—but not un-intelligibly—all the modes of Paracletic manifestation, among others, there-fore, the manifestation of the Prophet Mohammed, who was none other than the personification of the Paraclete or the cyclic manifestation of the latter; moreover, the Koran, like the appearance of the Holy Ghost at Pentecost, is called a "descent" (*tanzīl*). It may be added that if the second coming of Christ at the end of our cycle will have a universal significance for men, in the sense that it will concern the entire human race and not merely "a humanity" in the ordinary religious meaning of the word—the Paraclete itself, in its great apparition, had to manifest this universality by anticipation, at least in relation to the Christian world, and it is for that reason that the cyclic manifestation of the Paraclete, or its personification in Mohammed, had to appear outside Christianity in order to shatter a certain "particularist" limitation.

† Christ expressed this by saying that "God only is good." Inasmuch as the term "good" implies every possible positive meaning, and therefore every one of the Divine Qualities, the saying may also be taken to mean that "God alone is unique," which takes us to the doctrinal affirmation of Islam: "There is no divinity [or reality] if it is not the [one] Divinity [or Reality]." To any-one who would contest the legitimacy of this interpretaton of the Scriptures, we will answer with Meister Eckhart that "all truth is taught by the Holy Ghost; it is true that there is a literal meaning which the author had in mind, but since God is the Author of Holy Scripture, every true meaning is at the same time a literal meaning; for all that is true comes from the Truth itself, is contained in It, derives from It, and is willed by It." We may also quote a passage from Dante relating to the same subject:

The Scriptures can be understood and ought to be expounded according to four senses. The first is called the literal. . . . The fourth is called the anagogical, that

9

In the final analysis the relationship between exoterism and
esoterism is equivalent to the relationship between "form" and
"spirit" that is discoverable in all expressions and symbols; this
relationship must clearly also exist within esoterism itself, and it
may be said that only the spiritual authority places himself at the
level of naked and integral Truth. The "spirit," that is to say, the
supraformal content of the form, which, for its part, corresponds
to the "letter," always displays a tendency to breach its formal
limitations, thereby putting itself in apparent contradiction with
them. It is for this reason that one may consider every religious
readaptation, and therefore every Revelation, as fulfilling the function of an esoterism in relation to the preceding religious form;
Christianity, for example, is esoteric relatively to the Judaic form,
and Islam relatively to the Judaic and Christian forms, though this
is, of course, only valid when regarded from the special point of
view that we are here considering and would be quite false if understood literally. Moreover, insofar as Islam is distinguished by its
form from the other two monotheistic religions, that is to say,
insofar as it is formally limited, these religions also possess an
esoteric aspect relatively to it, and the same reversibility of relationship applies as between Christianity and Judaism. However,
the relationship to which we referred first is a more direct one than
the second, since it was Islam that, in the name of the spirit,
shattered the forms that preceded it, and Christianity that shattered
the Judaic form, and not the other way around. To return, however, to the purely principial consideration of the relationship between form and spirit, we cannot do better than quote, by way of
example, the following passage from the *Treatise on Unity* (*Risālat*

---

is to say, that which surpasses the senses [*sovrasenso*]; this occurs when one ex-
pounds spiritually a Scripture which, though true in the literal sense, also signifies
the higher things belonging to the eternal glory, as one may see in the Psalm of
the Prophet where it is said that when the people of Israel departed out of Egypt,
Judaea was made holy and free. Although this was clearly true according to the
letter, the spiritual meaning is no less true, namely, that when the soul departs
from sin, it is rendered holy and free in its power. [*Il Convito* 2.1]

al-Aḥadīyah) by Muḥyi 'd-Dīn ibn ʿArabī, which clearly illustrates the esoteric function of "shattering the form in the name of the spirit": "Most initiates say that the knowledge of Allāh follows upon the extinction of existence [*fanāʾ al-wujūd*] and the extinction of this extinction [*fanāʾ al-fanāʾ*]; but this opinion is entirely false. . . . Knowledge does not demand the extinction of existence [of the ego] or the extinction of this extinction; for things have no existence, and that which does not exist cannot cease to exist." Now the fundamental ideas that Ibn ʿArabī rejects, moreover with a purely speculative or methodic intention, are still accepted even by those who consider Ibn ʿArabī as the greatest of spiritual masters; and in an analogous manner all exoteric forms are transcended or shattered, and therefore in a certain sense denied, by esoterism, which is nevertheless the first to recognize the perfect legitimacy of every form of Revelation, being indeed alone competent to recognize this legitimacy.

"The wind bloweth where it listeth," and because of its universality shatters forms, though it must needs clothe itself in a form while on the formal plane.

"If you would have the Kernel," said Meister Eckhart, "you must break the husk."

Transcendence and Universality of Esoterism

1

Before coming to the main subject of this chapter, it is necessary that certain points regarding the more outward modes of esoterism should first of all be disposed of, though we would gladly have left this contingent aspect of the question out of account in order to concentrate solely on the essential; but since certain contingencies are liable to give rise to disputes about principles, there is really no alternative but to pause and consider them, a task that we shall try to carry out as briefly as possible.

One of the first things that may cause difficulty is the fact that although esoterism is reserved, by definition and because of its very nature, for an intellectual elite necessarily restricted in numbers, one cannot help observing that initiatory organizations have at all times included in their ranks a relatively large number of members. This was the case, for instance, with the Pythagoreans, and it is even more noticeable in the case of the initiatory orders that, despite their decadence, still exist today, such as the Moslem brotherhoods. Even where one finds a very exclusive initiatory organization, it is in nearly all cases a branch or nucleus of a very much larger brotherhood and does not constitute a complete brotherhood in itself, save for some exceptions that are always possible in particular circumstances. The explanation of this more or less "popular" participation in what is most inward and hence most subtle in a religion is that esoterism, in order to exist in a given world, must be integrated with a particular modality of that world, and this will necessarily involve relatively numerous elements of society; this leads to a distinction, within the brotherhoods, between inner and outer circles, the members of the latter being scarcely aware of the real nature of the organization to which they belong in a certain degree, and which they regard simply as a form of the outward religion, which alone is accessible to them. To return to the example of the Moslem brotherhoods, this is the explanation of the distinction made between those members who are merely characterized as *mutabārik* ("blessed" or "initiated") and whose viewpoint hardly extends beyond the exoteric perspective, which they wish to live with intensity, and members of the elite who have attained the degree of *sālik* ("one who travels") and follow the way marked out by the initiatory tradition; it is true that nowadays the number of genuine *sālikūn* is exceedingly small, whereas the *mutabārikūn* are far too numerous from the standpoint of the normal equilibrium of the brotherhoods and, by their manifold incomprehensions, contribute to the stifling of true spirituality. However that may be, the *mutabārikūn,* even when they are unable to understand the transcendent reality of the brotherhood that has received them, nonetheless derive, under normal conditions, a great benefit from the *barakah* ("benediction" or "spiritual influence") that surrounds and protects them according to the degree of their fervor; for it goes without saying that the radiation of grace within esoterism extends, by reason of the latter's very universality, through all the domains of the traditional civilization and is not halted by any formal limit, just as light, colorless in itself, is not halted by the color of a transparent body.

All the same, this participation of the "people," that is, of men representing the collective average, in the spirituality of the elite is not always to be explained solely by reasons of opportunity but also, and above all, by the law of polarity or compensation whereby "extremes meet," and it is for this reason also that "the voice of the people is the Voice of God" (*Vox populi, Vox Dei*); it may be said that the people, in their capacity as passive and unconscious transmitters of the symbols, represent, as it were, the periphery or the passive or feminine reflection of the elite, the latter possessing and transmitting the symbols in an active and conscious way. This also explains the curious and apparently paradoxical affinity existing between the people and the elite: for instance, Taoism is at the same time esoteric and popular, whereas Confucianism is exoteric and more or less aristocratic and "literate"; or, to take another example, the Sufi brotherhoods have always possessed a popular aspect that is to some extent correlative to their esoteric aspect. The reason for this lies in the fact that the people, in addition to their peripheral aspect, possess also an aspect of totality, and the latter corresponds analogically to the center. It can be said that the intellectual functions of the people are the crafts and folklore, the first representing method or realization and the second doctrine; in this way the people reflect, passively and collectively, the essential function of the elite, namely, the transmission of the properly intellectual aspect of the religion, a clothing for which is provided by symbolism in all its forms.

Another question that needs elucidating before we proceed any further concerns the idea of the universality of religion. This idea, being still of a more or less outward order, is clouded over by all sorts of historical and geographical contingencies, so much so that certain people freely doubt its existence; for instance, we have heard it disputed somewhere that Sufism admits this idea, and it has been argued that Muḥyi 'd-Dīn ibn 'Arabī denied it when he wrote that Islam was the pivot of the other religions. The truth is, however, that every religious form is superior to the others in a particular respect, and it is this characteristic that in fact indicates the sufficient reason for the existence of that form. Anyone who speaks in the name of his religion always has this characteristic in mind; what matters, where the recognition of other religious forms is concerned, is the fact—exoterically inconceivable—of such recognition, not its mode or degree. Moreover, this point of view finds its prototype in the Koran itself; in one place the Koran says that all the Prophets are equal, while elsewhere it declares that some are superior to others. This means, according to the commentary of Ibn 'Arabī, that each Prophet is superior to the others by reason of a particularity that is peculiar to him, and therefore in a certain respect. Ibn 'Arabī belonged to the Islamic civilization and owed his spiritual realization to the Islamic *barakah* and the Masters of Sufism, in a word, to the Islamic form of religion; he must needs, therefore, have placed himself at this point of view, that is to say, at the standpoint of the relationship wherein the Islamic form is superior by comparison with other forms. If this relative superiority did not exist, those Hindus who became Moslems through the centuries could have had no positive reason for acting as they did. The fact that Islam constitutes the last form of the *Sanātana Dharma* in this *mahā-yuga,* to use Hindu terms, implies that this form possesses a certain contingent superiority over preceding forms; similarly, the fact that Hinduism is the most ancient of the living religious forms implies that it possesses a certain superiority or centrality with respect to later forms. There is not, of course, any contradiction here, since the standpoint is different in the two cases.

In the same way, the fact that St. Bernard preached the Crusades and that he was probably ignorant of the real nature of Islam is in no wise inconsistent with his esoteric knowledge. The question is not whether St. Bernard did or did not understand Islam but whether he would have understood it had he enjoyed direct and regular contacts with this form of Revelation, in the same manner as it was understood by the Templar elite who found themselves in a position favorable to such understanding. A man's spirituality cannot be held to depend on knowledge of a historical or geographical kind or on any other "scientific" information of a similar order. It can therefore be said that the universalism of esoterists is virtual as to its possible applications and that it only becomes effective when circumstances permit or impose a determined application. In other words, it is only after contact with another civilization that this universalism is actualized, though there is, of course, no strict law governing this matter and the factors that will determine the acceptance by an esoterist of any particular alien form may vary greatly according to the case; it is clearly impossible to define exactly what constitutes a contact with an alien form, a contact, that is to say, that will be sufficient to bring about the understanding of such a form.*

2

We must now answer more explicitly the question as to the truths that exoterism must of necessity ignore, without, however, expressly denying them.[1] Perhaps the most important among the conceptions that are inaccessible to exoterism is, in certain respects at least, that of the gradation of universal Reality: Reality affirms itself by degrees, but without ceasing to be "one," the inferior degrees of

* An analogous remark may be made regarding the holy men known to Sufism by the name of *Afrād* ("solitary ones"; singular, *Fard*): these men who by definition have always been very few, are distinguished by the fact of possessing an effective initiation spontaneously, without having had to be initiated ritually. Such men, having obtained knowledge without studies or spiritual exercises of any sort, may well be ignorant of those things of which personally they have no need. Not having been initiated, they have no occasion to know what initiation means in the technical sense; thus they speak in the manner of men of the Golden Age—an epoch when initiation was not yet necessary—rather than in the manner of spiritual instructors of the Iron Age; moreover, since they have not followed a path of realization, they cannot assume the role of spiritual Master.

Similarly, if Shrī Ramakrishna was unable to foresee the deviation of some of his disciples, it was because his ignorance of the modern Western mentality made it impossible for him to interpret certain visions otherwise than in a normally Hindu sense. It must be added, however, that this deviation, which is of a doctrinal order and of modern Western inspiration, does not annul the influence of grace issuing from Shrī Ramakrishna, but is merely superimposed upon it in the manner of a superfluous decoration, nonexistent spiritually; in other words, the fact that the saint's *bhakti* has been travestied in a pseudo-*jnāna* in the philosophico-religious or European style in no way prevents the spiritual influence from being what it is. Similarly if Shrī Ramakrishna intended to bestow freely the radiation of his *bhakti* consistently with certain particular conditions connected with the end of the cycle, such an intention is independent of the forms that the zeal of some of his disciples came to take; moreover, this willingness to give generously of himself allies the saint of Dakshineswar to the spiritual family of Christ, so much so that everything that can be said of the particular nature of the spiritual radiation of Christ may also be applied to the radiation of the *Paramahamsa: Et lux in tenebris lucet, et tenebrae eam non comprehenderunt.*

1. Numbered notes start on page 139.

this affirmation being absorbed, by metaphysical integration or synthesis, into the superior degrees. This is the doctrine of the cosmic illusion: the world is not only more or less imperfect or ephemeral, but cannot even be said to "be" at all in relation to absolute Reality, since the reality of the world would limit God's Reality and He alone "is." Furthermore, Being Itself, which is none other than the Personal God, is in its turn surpassed by the Impersonal or Supra-Personal Divinity, Non-Being, of which the Personal God or Being is simply the first determination from which flow all the secondary determinations that make up cosmic Existence. Exoterism cannot, however, admit either this unreality of the world or the exclusive reality of the Divine Principle, or above all, the transcendence of Non-Being relative to Being or God. In other words, the exoteric point of view cannot comprehend the transcendence of the supreme Divine Impersonality of which God is the personal Affirmation; such truths are of too high an order, and therefore too subtle and too complex from the point of view of simple rational understanding, to be accessible to the majority or formulated in a dogmatic manner. Another idea that exoterism does not admit is that of the immanence in all beings of the Intellect, which Meister Eckhart defined as "uncreate and uncreatable";* clearly this truth cannot be integrated in the exoteric perspective any more than the idea of metaphysical realization, by which man becomes conscious of that which has never really ceased to be, namely, his essential identity with the Divine Principle that alone is real.† Exoterism, on the other hand, is obliged to maintain the

---

* It is common knowledge that certain passages from Eckhart's works that went beyond the theological point of view, and were therefore outside the competence of the religious authority as such, were condemned by this authority. If this verdict was nevertheless justifiable on grounds of expediency, it was certainly not so in its form, and by a curious repercussion John XXII, who had issued the Bull, was in his turn obliged to retract an opinion that he had preached, and saw his authority shaken. Eckhart only retracted in a purely principial manner, through simple obedience and before even knowing the papal decision; consequently his disciples were not disturbed by his retraction any more than they were by the Bull itself. We may add that one of them, Blessed Henry Suso, had a vision after Eckhart's death of the "Blessed Master, deified in God in a superabundant magnificence."

† The Sufi Yaḥyā Muʿādh ar-Rāzī said that "Paradise is the prison of the

distinction between Lord and servant, leaving aside the fact that the profanely minded affect to see in the metaphysical idea of essential identity nothing but "pantheism," which incidentally relieves them of any effort at comprehension.

This idea of "pantheism" warrants a further short digression. In reality, pantheism consists in the admission of a continuity between the Infinite and the finite; but this continuity can only be conceived if it is first admitted that there is a substantial identity between the ontological Principle—which is in question in all forms of theism—and the manifested order, a conception that presupposes a substantial, and therefore false, idea of Being, or the confusing of the essential identity of manifestation and Being with a substantial identity. Pantheism is this and nothing else; it seems, however, that some minds are incurably obstinate when faced with so simple a truth, unless it be that they are impelled by some passion or

---

initiate as the world is the prison of the believer"; in other words, universal manifestation (*al-khalq,* or the Hindu *samsāra*), including its beatific Center (*As-Samawāt* or the *Brahma-Loka*) is metaphysically an (apparent) limitation (of the nonmanifested Reality: Allāh, Brahma), just as formal manifestation is a limitation (of the supraformal, but still manifested, Reality: *As-Samawāt, Brahma-Loka*) from an individual or exoteric point of view. However, such a formulation is exceptional; esoterism is in general implicit and not explicit, finding its normal expression through the medium of the Scriptural symbols; thus, to take Sufism as an example, the word "Paradise" adopted from the Koranic terminology is employed to denote states, such as the "Paradise of the Essence" (*Jannat adh-Dhāt*), that are situated beyond every cosmic reality and, for still stronger reasons, beyond every individual determination. If, therefore, a Sufi refers to "Paradise" as the prison of the initiate, he is merely considering it from the ordinary and cosmic point of view, which is that of the exoteric perspective, as he is obliged to do when he wishes to show the essential difference between the individual and universal or cosmic and metacosmic ways. It must therefore never be forgotten that the "Kingdom of Heaven" of the Gospels and the "Paradise" (*Jannah*) of the Koran, do not represent only conditioned states, but also, and simultaneously, aspects of the Unconditioned State of which they are only the most direct cosmic reflections.

To return to the quotation from Yaḥyā Mu'ādh ar-Rāzī, we find an analogous idea expressed in the condemned passages from Meister Eckhart: "Those who seek neither fortune, nor honors, nor benefits, nor inward devotion, nor saintliness, nor recompense, nor the Kingdom of Heaven, but have renounced all, even that which is their own, it is in these men that God is glorified." This sentence, like that of Ar-Rāzī's, expresses the metaphysical negation of the individuality in the realization of the Supreme Identity.

interest not to let go of such a convenient polemical instrument as the term "pantheism," the use of which allows them to cast a general suspicion over certain doctrines that are considered embarrassing, without involving them in the trouble of examining the doctrines in themselves.* Even if the idea of God were no more than a conception of the universal Substance (*materia prima*), and the ontological Principle were therefore in no way involved, the reproach of pantheism would still be unjustified, inasmuch as the *materia prima* always remains transcendent and virginal in relation to its productions. If God is conceived as primordial Unity, that is, as pure Essence, nothing could be substantially identical with Him; to qualify essential identity as pantheistic is both to deny the relativity of things and to attribute an autonomous reality to them in relation to Being or Existence, as if there could be two realities essentially distinct, or two Unities or Unicities. The fatal consequence of such reasoning is pure and simple materialism, for once manifestation is no longer conceived as being essentially identical with its Principle, the logical admission of this Principle becomes solely a question of credulity, and if this sentimental reason collapses there is no longer any reason for admitting the existence of anything beyond manifestation, and more particularly, beyond sensory manifestation.

3

Let us now return to the subject of the Divine Impersonality to which reference has already been made. Strictly speaking, this

---

* Pantheism is the great resource of all those who want to brush aside esoterism with the minimum of inconvenience and who, for example, imagine that they can understand a given metaphysical or initiatory text because they know the grammar of the language in which it is written. What can one say of all those treatises that attempt to make the religious doctrines a subject of profane study, as if there were no knowledge that was not accessible to anybody and everybody and as if it were sufficient to have been to school to be able to understand the most venerable wisdom better than the sages understood it themselves? For it is assumed by "specialists" and "critics" that there is nothing that is beyond their powers; such an attitude resembles that of children who, having found books intended for adults, judge them according to their ignorance, caprice, or laziness.

"Impersonality" is more properly a "Non-Personality," that is to say, it is neither personal nor impersonal but suprapersonal. In any case, the term "Impersonality" should not be understood in a privative sense, for, on the contrary, it refers here to an absolute Plenitude and Illimitability that is determined by nothing, not even by Itself. It is Personality that represents a sort of privation, or rather privative determination relative to Impersonality, and not the reverse. Needless to say, the term "Personality," as it is used here, must be taken to refer only to the Personal God or "Divine Ego," if one may use such an expression, and not to the "Self," which is the transcendent principle of the individual ego and which may be called the Personality relative to the individuality without any limitation being thereby implied. The distinction we are concerned with here is therefore between the Divine Person, principial Prototype of the individuality on the one hand, and the Divine Impersonality, which is, so to speak, the infinite Essence of this Person, on the other. This distinction between the Divine Person, who manifests a particular Will in a given "world," symbolically unique, and the Divine "impersonal" Reality, which, on the contrary, manifests the essential and universal Divine Will through the forms of the particular or personal Divine Will—and sometimes in apparent contradiction with the latter—this distinction, we repeat, is absolutely fundamental in esoterism, not only because it is an important feature of metaphysical doctrine, but also, secondarily, because it explains the antinomy that may appear to exist between the exoteric and esoteric spheres. For example, in the case of the Prophet Solomon, we must distinguish between his esoteric knowledge, which may be referred to what we have called, for lack of a better term, the "Divine Impersonality," and his exoteric orthodoxy, that is to say, his conformity to the Will of the "Divine Person"; it was not by virtue of opposition to this Will but by reason of the aforementioned knowledge that the great builder of the Temple of Yahweh recognized the Divinity in other revealed forms, even though these were in a state of decadence. Consequently it was not the decadence or paganism of these forms that he accepted but their primitive purity that was still recognizable in their symbolism, so that he may be said to have accepted them despite the veil of their decadence; moreover, is not the insistence of the Book of Wisdom on the vanity of idolatry a sort of contradiction of the exoteric interpretation of Solomon's attitude given in the Book of Kings? However that may be, Solomon, while being in himself superior to particular forms, nevertheless had to suffer the consequences of the contradictions to which his universalism gave rise on the formal plane. The Bible essentially affirms one form, that of Judaic monotheism, and does so in the particularly "formal" mode of historical symbolism, which, by definition, is concerned with events; it must therefore blame Solomon's attitude insofar as it was in contradiction with the Personal manifestation of the Divinity, yet at the same time it infers that the person of the Sage himself was unaffected by the infraction.* Solomon's "irregular" attitude brought political schism to his kingdom; this is the only sanction recorded by the Scriptures, and it would be a quite disproportionate punishment if the Prophet-King had really practiced polytheism, which, in fact, he never did. The sanction mentioned above took effect exactly on the level at which the irregularity had occurred, and not above it; moreover, Solomon's memory has continued to be venerated not only in Judaism, particularly in the Kabbalah, but also in Islam, Sharaite as well as Sufic; as for Christianity, one need only recall the commentaries that have been inspired by the Song of Songs, for example, those of St. Gregory of Nyssa, Theodoret, and St. Bernard. It remains to be said that if the antinomy between the two principal dimensions of religion arises in the Bible itself, notwithstanding that it is a Sacred Book, this is because the mode of expression of this Book,

* Thus, the Koran affirms that "Solomon was not impious" (or "heretical": mā kafara Sulaymān [Sūrat al-Baqarah, 102]) and exalts him in these words: "How excellent a servant was Solomon! Verily, he was always [in spirit] turned towards Allāh" (the commentators add: "Glorifying Him and praising Him without ceasing" [Sūrat Ṣād, 30]). Nevertheless, the Koran alludes to an ordeal imposed on Solomon by God, then to a prayer of repentance uttered by the Prophet-King, and lastly to the Divine hearing of this prayer (ibid., 34–36). The commentary on this enigmatic passage accords symbolically with the narrative in the Book of Kings, since it records that one of Solomon's wives, without his knowledge and in his own palace, adored an idol; Solomon lost his seal and, with it, his kingdom for several days, then found the seal again and recovered his kingdom; he then prayed to God to pardon him and obtained from Him a greater and more marvelous power than he had had before.

like the Judaic form itself, gives preponderance to the exoteric point of view—one might almost say social, or even political, though not, of course, in the profane sense. In Christianity, on the other hand, the relationship is reversed, while in Islam, which is a synthesis of the Judaic and Christian "geniuses," the two religious dimensions appear side by side in equilibrium; as to the Koran, it only considers Solomon (*Sayyidnā Sulaymān*) in his esoteric aspect and in the capacity of Prophet.* Lastly, let us quote a passage from the Bible in which Yahweh orders the Prophet Nathan to repeat the following words to David:

And when thy days be fulfilled, and thou shalt sleep with thy fathers, I will set up thy seed after thee, which [Solomon] shall proceed out of

---

* The sacred book of Islam expresses the impeccability of the Prophets as follows: "They do not take precedence over Him [Allāh] in their speech [they do not speak first] and they act according to His commandments" (*Sūrat al-Anbiyā'*, 27); this amounts to saying that the Prophets do not speak without inspiration or act without the Divine commandment. This impeccability is compatible with the "imperfect actions" (*dhunūb*) of the Prophets only by virtue of the metaphysical truth of the two Divine Realities, one "personal" and the other "impersonal," the respective manifestations of which may contradict each other on the level of facts, at least in the case of the great saints, though never in the case of ordinary mortals. The word *dhanb*, though it also means "sin" and particularly "unintentional sin," primarily and originally means "imperfection in action" or "imperfection resulting from an action"; that is why the word *dhanb* is used when it refers to the Prophets and not the word *ithm*, which signifies exclusively "sin" with emphasis on its intentional character. If one were to insist on seeing a contradiction between the impeccability of the Prophets and the extrinsic imperfection of some of their actions one would also have to admit an incompatibility between the perfection of Christ and his words regarding his human nature: "Why call you me good? God only is good." These words also answer the question as to why David and Solomon did not foresee conflict with a particular degree of the universal Law: the answer being that the individual nature always retains certain "blind spots" the presence of which enters into its very definition. It goes without saying that this necessary limitation of every individual substance in no way affects the spiritual reality to which this substance is joined in a quasi-accidental manner, since there is no common measure between the individual and the spiritual, the latter being synonymous with the Divine.

Lastly we will quote the following words of the Caliph Ali, the representative *par excellence* of Islamic esoterism: "To whomsoever narrates the story of David as the story tellers narrate it [that is, with an exoteric or profane interpretation], I will give one hundred and sixty lashes, and this will be the punishment of those who bear false witness against the Prophets."

thy bowels, and I will establish his Kingdom. He shall build an house for my name, and I will establish the throne of his Kingdom for ever. I will be his father and he shall be my son. If he commit iniquity, I will chasten him with the rod of men, and with the stripes of the children of men: but my mercy shall not depart away from him as I took it from Saul whom I put away before thee. [2 Sam. 7:12-15]

An analogous example is that of David, whom the Koran also recognizes as a Prophet and whom Christians recognize as one of the greatest saints of the Old Covenant. It is clear that a saint cannot commit the sins (note that we do not say "accomplish the actions") with which David is reproached. What needs to be understood is that the "transgression" that the Bible, in conformity with its "legal" point of view, attributes to the saintly King appears as such only because of the essentially moral, and therefore exoteric, perspective that predominates in this Sacred Book (which explains the attitude of St. Paul and of Christianity in general toward Judaism, the Christian point of view being eminently "inward") whereas the impeccability of the Prophets, as affirmed for example by the Koran, corresponds, on the contrary, to a deeper reality than can be attained by the moral point of view. Esoterically, David's desire to marry Bathsheba could not be a transgression, since the quality of Prophet can only attach to men who are free from passions, whatever may be the appearances in certain cases. What must be discerned above all in the relationship between David and Bathsheba is an affinity or cosmic and providential complementarism, of which the fruit and justification was Solomon, he whom "Yahweh loved" (2 Sam. 7:25). The coming of this second Prophet-King was a Divine confirmation of, and a benediction on, the union between David and Bathsheba, and God does not authorize or recompense transgression. According to Muḥyi 'd-Dīn ibn 'Arabī, Solomon represented for David more than a recompense: "Solomon was the gift of Allāh to David, in conformity with the Divine Words: and we gave Solomon to David as a gift [Koran, Sūrat Ṣād, 30]. Now one receives a gift through favor and not as a reward of merit; it is for this reason that Solomon is the overflowing grace, the clear proof and the mighty blow." (Fuṣūṣ al-Ḥikam, Kalimah Sulaymānīyah.)

Let us now consider the story insofar as it concerns Uriah the Hittite; here no less, David's manner of acting should not be judged according to the moral point of view, since, quite apart from the fact that a heroic death with face turned toward the enemy is very far from prejudicial to the last ends of a warrior, and that when it occurs, as here, in a Holy War, such a death possesses an immediate sacrificial character, the motive behind this manner of acting could only be a Prophetic intuition. However, the choice of Bathsheba and the sending of Uriah to his death, although cosmologically and providentially justified, nonetheless clashed with the exoteric Law, and David, while benefiting, by Solomon's birth, from the intrinsic legitimacy of his action, had to bear the consequences of this clash; but the very fact that an echo of the clash appears in the Psalms, which is a Sacred Book because Divinely inspired—its existence proving, moreover, that David was a Prophet—shows once again that David's actions, though having a negative aspect on an outward plane, nevertheless do not constitute "sins" in themselves. One might even say that God inspired these actions with a view to the Revelation of the Psalms, of which the purpose was to record, in Divine and immortal song, not only the sufferings and glory of the soul in search of God, but also the sufferings and glory of the Messiah. David's manner of acting was clearly not in all respects contrary to the Divine Will, since God not only "pardoned" David (to use the somewhat anthropomorphic biblical term), but even allowed him to keep Bathsheba, the cause and object of the "sin." Furthermore, not only did God not take Bathsheba away from David, but He even confirmed their union by the gift of Solomon; and if it is true, for David as well as for Solomon, that the outward or purely extrinsic irregularity of certain actions provoked a corresponding reaction, it is important to recognize that this reaction was strictly limited to the terrestrial domain. These two aspects, the one outward or negative and the other inward or positive, of the history of Uriah's wife, again find expression in two other facts: firstly, the death of her first-born, and secondly, the life, greatness, and glory of her second son, he whom "Yahweh loved."

This digression was necessary in order to bring out more clearly the profoundly different natures of the exoteric and esoteric domains and to show that whenever there is incompatibility between them it can only spring from the first and never from the second, which is superior to forms and therefore beyond all oppositions. There is a Sufic formula that illustrates as clearly and concisely as possible the different viewpoints of the two great ways: "The exoteric way: I and Thou. The esoteric way: I am Thou and Thou art I. Esoteric knowledge: neither I nor Thou, Him."

Exoterism may be said to be founded on the "creature-Creator" dualism to which it attributes an absolute reality, as though the Divine Reality, which is metaphysically unique, did not absorb or annul the relative reality of the creature and hence any and every relative and apparently extradivine reality. While it is true that esoterism also admits the distinction between the individual ego and the universal or Divine Self, it does so only in a provisional and "methodic" manner and not in an absolute sense; taking its point of departure at the level of this duality, which obviously corresponds to a relative reality, it ultimately passes beyond it metaphysically, which would be impossible from the exoteric point of view, the limitation of which consists precisely in its attributing an absolute reality to what is contingent. This brings us to what is really the definition of the exoteric perspective, namely, an irreducible dualism and the exclusive pursuit of individual salvation—this dualism implying that God is considered solely under the aspect of His relationship with the created and not in His total and infinite Reality, in His Impersonality which annihilates all apparent reality other than Him.

It is not the actual fact of this dogmatic dualism that is blameworthy, since it corresponds exactly to the individual viewpoint at which religion places itself, but solely the inductions that imply the attribution of an absolute reality to what is relative. Metaphysically, human reality is reducible to the Divine Reality and in itself is only illusory; theologically, Divine Reality is in appearance reduced to human reality, in the sense that It does not surpass the latter in existential but only in causal quality.

4

The perspective of the esoteric doctrines shows up with particular clarity in their way of regarding what is commonly called "evil"; it has often been said that they deny evil purely and simply, but such an interpretation is too rudimentary and expresses the perspective of the doctrines in question in a very imperfect manner. The difference between the religious and metaphysical conceptions of evil does not mean, moreover, that the one is false and the other true, but simply that the former is incomplete and individual whereas the latter is integral and universal; what the exoteric perspective represents as evil or the Devil only corresponds therefore to a partial view and is in no way the equivalent of the negative cosmic tendency that is envisaged by the metaphysical doctrines, and which Hindu doctrine designates by the term *tamas;* but if *tamas* is not the Devil, and more correctly corresponds to the Demiurge, insofar as it represents the cosmic tendency that "solidifies" manifestation, drawing it downward and away from its Principle and Origin, it is nonetheless true that the Devil is a form of *tamas,* the latter being considered in this case solely in its relations with the human soul. Man being a conscious individual, the cosmic tendency in question, when it comes in contact with him, necessarily takes on an individual and conscious aspect, a "personal" aspect, according to the current expression. Outside the human world this same tendency may assume entirely impersonal and neutral aspects, as, for example, when it is manifested as physical weight or material density, or in the guise of a hideous beast or of a common and heavy metal such as lead. The exoteric perspective, by definition, occupies itself only with man and considers cosmology solely in relation to him, so that there is no reason to reproach religion for considering *tamas* under a personified aspect, that is to say, under the aspect that actually touches the world of men. If, therefore, esoterism seems to deny evil, it is not because it ignores or refuses to recognize the nature of things as they are in reality; on the contrary, it completely penetrates their nature, and that is the reason why it is impossible for it to abstract from the cosmic reality one or other of its aspects or to consider one such aspect solely from the point of view of individual human interest. It is self-evident that the cosmic tendency of which the Devil is the quasi-human personification is not evil, since it is this same tendency, for example, that condenses material bodies, and if it were to disappear—an absurd supposition—all bodies or physical and psychic compositions would instantaneously volatilize. Even the most sacred object therefore has need of this tendency in order to be enabled to exist materially, and no one would be so rash as to assert that the physical law that condenses the material mass of, say, the Sacred Host is a diabolical force or in any sense an evil. It is precisely because of this neutral character (independent of the distinction between good and evil) of the demiurgic tendency that the esoteric doctrines, which reduce everything to its essential reality, seem to deny what in human parlance bears the name of "evil."

It may nevertheless be asked what consequences such a non-moral—we do not say "immoral"—conception of evil implies for the esoterist; the reply to this is that in the consciousness of the esoterist, and consequently in his life, "sin" is replaced by "dissipation," that is, by everything that is opposed to spiritual concentration or, in other words, to unity. Needless to say, the difference here is primarily one of principle and of method, and this difference does not affect all individuals in the same way; however, what morally is "sin" is nearly always "dissipation" from the initiatory point of view. This concentration—or tendency toward unity (tawḥīd)—becomes, in Islamic exoterism, faith in the Unity of God, and the greatest transgression is to associate other divinities with Allāh; for the initiate (the faqīr), on the other hand, this transgression will have a universal bearing in the sense that every purely individual affirmation will be tainted with this aspect of false divinity, and if, from the religious point of view, the greatest merit lies in the sincere profession of Divine Unity, the faqīr will realize this profession in a spiritual manner, giving to it a meaning that embraces all the orders of the universe, and this will be achieved precisely by the concentration of his whole being on the one Divine Reality. To make clearer this analogy between sin and dissipation we may take as an example the reading of a good book.

From the exoteric point of view this will never be considered as a reprehensible act, but it may be considered incidentally so in esoterism in cases where it amounts to a dissipation, or when the dissipation entailed by the act outweighs its usefulness. Inversely, a thing that would nearly always be considered by religious morality as a "temptation," and hence as a first step on the path to sin, may sometimes play the opposite part in esoterism, inasmuch as, far from being a dissipation, "sinful" or otherwise, it may be a factor of concentration by virtue of the immediate intelligibility of its symbolism. There are even cases, in Tantrism, for example, and in certain cults of antiquity, where acts that in themselves would count as sins, not only according to a particular religious morality but also according to the legislation of the civilization in which they occur, serve as a support for intellection, a fact that presupposes a strong predominance of the contemplative element over the passionate; however, a religious morality is never made for the benefit of contemplatives only but for that of all men.

It will be understood that we are far from depreciating morality, which is a Divine institution, but the fact that it is so does not prevent its being limited. It must be stated once again that in the majority of cases, moral laws, when transposed outside their ordinary sphere, become symbols and consequently vehicles of knowledge; in fact, every virtue is the mark of a conformity with a Divine attitude and therefore an indirect and quasi-existential mode of the knowledge of God, which amounts to saying that whereas a sensible object can be known by the eye, God can be known only by "being"; to know God it is necessary to resemble Him, that is, to conform the microcosm to the Divine Metacosm—and consequently to the macrocosm also—as is expressly taught by the Hesychast doctrine. That having been said, it is necessary strongly to underline the fact that the amorality of the spiritual position is rather a supermorality than a nonmorality. Morality, in the widest sense of the term, is in its own order a reflection of true spirituality and must be integrated, together with partial truths—or partial errors—in the total being; in other words, just as the most holy man is never entirely liberated from action on this earth, since he has a body, so he is never entirely liberated from the distinction between good and evil, since this distinction necessarily insinuates itself into every action.

Before considering the question of the actual existence of evil, we will add the following: the two great religious dimensions—exoterism and esoterism—can be, if not defined, at least described to some extent by associating with the former the terms "morality," "action," "merit," "grace," and with the latter the terms "symbolism," "concentration," "knowledge," "identity"; thus the passional man will approach God through action supported by a moral code, while the contemplative, on the other hand, will become united with his Divine Essence through concentration supported by a symbolism, without, of course, this excluding the former attitude within the limits that are proper to it. Morality is a principle of action, therefore of merit, whereas symbolism is a support of contemplation and a means of intellection; merit, which is acquired by a mode of action, has for its goal the Grace of God, whereas the goal of intellection, insofar as the latter can be distinguished from its goal, is union or identity with That which we have never ceased to be in our existential and intellectual Essence; in other words, the supreme goal is the reintegration of man in the Divinity, of the contingent in the Absolute, of the finite in the Infinite. Morality as such obviously has no meaning outside the relatively very restricted domain of action and merit, and therefore in no way extends to such realities as symbolism, contemplation, intellection, and identity through knowledge. As for moralism, which must not be confused with morality, this is merely the tendency to substitute the moral point of view for all other points of view; it has the result, in Christianity at least, of fostering a kind of prejudice or suspicion with regard to anything of an agreeable nature, as well as the erroneous notion that all pleasant things are only that and nothing more. It is forgotten that for the true contemplative the positive quality and hence the symbolic and spiritual value of such things will greatly outweigh any disadvantage that may arise from a temporary indulgence of human nature, for every positive quality is essentially—though not existentially—identified with a Divine quality or perfection that is its eternal and infinite prototype. If in the foregoing remarks there is some appearance of contradiction, this is due to the fact that we have considered morality first of all as it is in itself, that is to say, as a matter of social or psychological expediency, and secondly as a symbolic element, therefore in the quality of a support for intellection; in the latter case, the opposition between morality and symbolism (or intellectuality) is obviously meaningless.

Now, as regards the problem of the existence of evil itself, the religious point of view gives only an indirect and somewhat evasive answer, declaring that the Divine Will is unfathomable, and that out of all evil good will ultimately come. This second proposition does not, however, explain evil, and as for the first, to say that God is unfathomable means that there is some appearance of contradiction in His ways that we are unable to resolve. From an esoteric point of view the problem of evil resolves itself into two questions: firstly, why do things created necessarily imply imperfection? and secondly, why do they exist? To the first of these questions the answer is that if there were no imperfection in the Creation nothing would distinguish it from the Creator, or in other words, it would not be effect or manifestation, but Cause or Principle; the answer to the second question is that the Creation (or Manifestation) is necessarily implied in the infinity of the Principle, in the sense that it is so to speak an aspect or consequence of this infinity. This amounts to saying that if the world did not exist the Infinite would not be the Infinite; to be what It is, the Infinite must apparently and symbolically deny Itself, and this denial is achieved in universal Manifestation. The world cannot but exist, since it is a possible and therefore necessary aspect of the absolute necessity of Being; imperfection, no less, cannot but exist, since it is an aspect of the very existence of the world. The existence of the world is strictly implied in the infinity of the Divine Principle, and the existence of evil is similarly implied in the existence of the world. God is All-Goodness, and the world is His image; but since the image cannot, by definition, be That which it represents, the world must be limited relatively to the Divine Goodness, hence the imperfection in existence. Imperfections may therefore be likened to fissures in the image of the Divine All-Perfection, and their origin is clearly to be sought not in this Perfection itself but in the necessarily relative or secondary character of the image. Manifestation implies imperfection by definition, as the Infinite implies Manifestation by definition. This triad "Infinite-Manifestation-imperfection" provides the formula that explains everything that the human mind may find problematical in the vicissitudes of existence; those who with the eye of the Intellect are capable of viewing the metaphysical causes of all appearances will never find themselves brought to a standstill by insoluble contradictions, as necessarily happens to those limited to an exoteric perspective, which, by reason of its anthropomorphism, can never hope to grasp all the aspects of universal Reality.

5

Another example of the helplessness of the human mind when left to its own resources is the problem of predestination. This idea of predestination is simply an expression, in the language of human ignorance, of the Divine Knowledge that in its perfect simultaneity embraces all possibilities without any restriction. In other words, if God is omniscient He knows future events, or rather events that appear thus to beings limited by time; if God did not know these events He would not be omniscient; from the moment that He knows them they appear as predestined relative to the individual. The individual will is free insofar as it is real; if it were not in any degree or in any way free it would be deprived of all reality; and in fact, compared with absolute Liberty, it has no reality, or more precisely, it is totally nonexistent. From the individual standpoint, however, which is the standpoint of human beings, the will is real in the measure in which they participate in the Divine Liberty, from which individual liberty derives all its reality by virtue of the causal relationship between the two; whence it follows that liberty, like all positive qualities, is Divine in itself and human insofar as it is not perfectly itself, in the same way that a reflection of the sun is identical with the sun, not as reflection but as light, light being one and indivisible in its essence.

The metaphysical link between predestination and liberty might be illustrated by comparing the latter to a liquid that settles into all the convolutions of a mold, the latter representing predestination: in that case the movement of the liquid is equivalent to the free exercise of our will. If we cannot will anything other than what is predestined for us, this does not prevent our will being what it is, namely, a relatively real participation in its universal prototype; it is precisely by means of this participation that we feel and live our will as being free.

The life of a man, and by extension the whole individual cycle of which that life and the human state itself are only modalities, is in fact contained in the Divine Intellect as a complete whole, that is to say, as a determined possibility that, being what it is, is not in any of its aspects other than itself, since a possibility is nothing else than an expression of the absolute necessity of Being; hence the unity or homogeneity of every possibility, which is accordingly something that cannot not be. To say that an individual cycle is included as a definitive formula in the Divine Intellect comes to the same thing as saying that a possibility is included in the Total Possibility, and it is this truth that furnishes the most decisive answer to the question of predestination. The individual will appears in this light as a process that realizes in successive mode the necessary interconnection of the modalities of its initial possibility, which is thus symbolically described or recapitulated. It can also be said that since the possibility of a being is necessarily a possibility of manifestation, the cyclic process of that being is the sum of the aspects of his manifestation and therefore of his possibility, and that the being, through the exercise of his will, merely manifests in deferred mode his simultaneous cosmic manifestation; in other words, the individual retraces in an analytic way his synthetic and primordial possibility, which, for its part, occupies a necessary place in the hierarchy of possibilities, the necessity of each possibility, as we have seen, being based metaphysically on the absolute necessity of the Divine All-Possibility.

6

In order to grasp the universality of esoterism, which is the same thing as the universality of metaphysic, it is important above all to understand that the means or organ of metaphysical knowledge is itself of a universal order and not, like reason, of an individual order; consequently this means or organ, which is the Intellect, must be found in all orders of nature and not only in man, as is the case with discursive thought. To answer the question as to how the Intellect is manifested in the peripheral domains of nature we shall have to introduce ideas that may prove somewhat puzzling for those who are unaccustomed to metaphysical and cosmological speculation, although, in themselves, these ideas represent fundamental and obvious truths. It may be said, therefore, that to the extent to which a state of existence is removed from the central state of the world to which it belongs—and the human state, like every other cosmologically analogous state, is central in relation to all peripheral states, whether terrestrial or not, and therefore not only in relation to the animal, vegetable, and mineral states but also to the angelic states, whence the adoration of Adam by the angels mentioned in the Koran—to the extent to which a state is peripheral, the Intellect becomes identified with its content, in the sense that a plant is even less able than an animal to know its own wishes or progress in knowledge, but is passively tied to and even identified with such knowledge as is imposed on it by its nature and that essentially determines its form. In other words, the form of a peripheral being, whether it be animal, vegetable, or mineral, reveals all that that being knows, and is, as it were, itself identified with this knowledge; it can be said, therefore, that the form of such a being gives a true indication of its contemplative state or dream. That which differentiates beings, in the measure in which they occupy states that are progressively more passive or unconscious, is their mode of knowledge or their intelligence. Humanly speaking it would be absurd to say that gold is more intelligent than copper or that lead has little intelligence, but metaphysically there is nothing ridiculous in such an assertion: gold represents a solar state of knowledge, and it is this, moreover, which permits of its association with spiritual influences and its being thus invested with an eminently sacred character. Needless to say, the object of knowledge or of intelligence is always and by definition the Divine Principle and cannot be anything else, since It is metaphysically the only Reality; but this object or content can vary in form in conformity with the indefinite diversity of the modes and degrees of Intelligence reflected in creatures. Furthermore, it must be pointed out that the manifested or created world has a double root, Existence and Intelligence, to which heat and light correspond analogically in igneous bodies; all beings and all things reveal these two aspects of relative reality. As already stated, that which differentiates beings and things is their mode and degree of intelligence; on the other hand, that which unites them is their existence, which is the same for all. But the relationship is reversed if we turn from the cosmic and horizontal continuity of the elements of the manifested world and consider their vertical connection with their transcendent Principle: that which unites the being, and more particularly the realized being, to the Divine Principle, is the Intellect; that which separates the world—or any microcosm—from the Principle, is Existence. In the case of man, intelligence is inward and existence outward; and since the latter does not in itself admit of differentiation, men form one single species, whereas differences of caste and spirituality are most marked. In the case of a being belonging to a peripheral domain, on the other hand, it is existence that is inward, since its lack of differentiation does not appear in the foreground, while intelligence or the mode of intellection is outward, differentiation appearing in the forms themselves, whence the endless diversity of species in all these domains. One might also say that man is normally, by primordial definition, pure knowledge and the mineral pure existence: the diamond, which stands at the summit of the mineral realm, integrates intelligence as such in its existence or manifestation, therefore passively and unconsciously, whence its hardness, transparency, and luminosity; the spiritually great man, who stands at the summit of the human species, integrates the whole of existence in his knowledge, therefore in an active and conscious manner, whence his universality.

7

The exoteric denial of the presence, whether virtual or actualized, of the uncreated Intellect in the created being, finds its most usual expression in the erroneous affirmation that no supernatural knowledge is possible apart from Revelation. But it is quite arbitrary to maintain that on this earth we have no immediate knowledge of God, and in fact that it is impossible for us to have such knowledge. This provides one more example of the opportunism that, on the one hand, denies the reality of the Intellect, and on the other hand, denies to those who enjoy the possession of it the right to know what it causes them to know. The reasons behind this denial are, firstly, that direct participation in what may be called the Paracletic faculty is not accessible to everybody, at least in practice, and secondly, that the doctrine of the presence of the uncreated Intellect in the creature would be prejudicial to the faith of the ordinary person, since it seems to run counter to the perspective of merit. What the exoteric point of view cannot admit, in Islam no less than in Christianity and Judaism, is the quasi-natural existence of a supernatural faculty, one that Christian dogma however admits with regard to Christ. It is apparently forgotten that the distinction between the supernatural and the natural is not absolute—unless in the sense of being "relatively absolute"—and that the supernatural can also be called natural insofar as it acts in accordance with certain laws. Inversely, the natural is not without a supernatural aspect insofar as it manifests the Divine Reality. Failing this, Nature would amount to pure nothingness. On the other hand, to maintain that the supernatural Knowledge of God, that is to say, the beatific vision in the next world, is an unobscured knowledge of the Divine Essence that is enjoyed by the individual soul, amounts to saying that absolute Knowledge can be achieved by a relative being as such, whereas, in reality, this Knowledge, being absolute, is none other than the Absolute insofar as It knows Itself; and if the Intellect, supernaturally present in man, can make man participate in this Knowledge that the Divinity has of Itself, it is because of certain Laws that are, so to speak, freely obeyed by the supernatural by virtue of its very possibilities. Again, if the supernatural differs in an eminent degree from the natural, it is nevertheless true that this difference no longer exists from another and more universal standpoint, that is to say, insofar as the supernatural itself also obeys—and is the first to obey—immutable Laws.

Knowledge is essentially holy (how else could Dante have spoken of the "venerable authority of the Philosopher"?) with a holiness that is truly Paracletic: "For to know thee is perfect righteousness," says the Book of Wisdom (15:3), and "to know thy power is the root of immortality." This saying is of the greatest doctrinal significance, being one of the clearest and most explicit formulations that can be found of the idea of realization by Knowledge, or in other words, of the intellectual way that leads to this Paracletic sanctity. In other sayings of equal excellence this same Book of Solomon enunciates the qualities of pure intellectuality, essence of all spirituality; the passage that follows, in addition to the marvelous metaphysical and initiatory precision of its expression, brings out in a remarkable manner the universal unity of Truth, and this is achieved by the very form of the language, which recalls partly the Scriptures of India and partly those of Taoism:

For in her [wisdom] is an understanding spirit, holy, one only, manifold, subtile, lively, clear, undefiled, plain, not subject to hurt, loving the thing that is good, quick, which cannot be letted, ready to do good, kind to man, steadfast, sure, free from care, having all power, overseeing all things, and going through all understanding, pure and most subtile spirits. For wisdom is more moving than any motion: she passeth and goeth through all things by reason of her pureness. For she is the breath of the power of God, and a pure influence flowing from the glory of the Almighty: therefore can no defiled thing fall into her. For she is the brightness of the everlasting light, the unspotted mirror of the power of God, and the image of his goodness. And being but one, she can do all things: and remaining in herself, she maketh all things new: and in all ages entering into holy souls, she maketh them friends of God, and prophets. For God loveth none but him that dwelleth with wisdom. For she is more beautiful than the sun, and above all the order of stars: being compared with the light, she is found before it. For after this cometh night: but vice shall not prevail against wisdom. Wisdom reacheth from one end to another mightily; and sweetly doth she order all things. [Wisd. of Sol. 7:22–30; 8:1]

In conclusion a word must be said to forestall a rather common objection. Certain people readily regard transcendent intelligence that is aware of itself as "pride," as if the fact that there are fools who believe themselves to be intelligent ought to prevent the wise from knowing what they know; pride, intellectual or otherwise, is only possible in the case of the ignorant, who are unaware of their own nothingness, just as humility, at least in the purely psychological sense of the term, is without meaning except for those who believe themselves to be something they are not. Those who wish to explain everything that is beyond them as pride, which to their way of thinking is the complement of "pantheism," manifestly ignore the fact that if God has created such souls in order to be known and realized by them and in them, man has no part in the matter and can do nothing to alter it; wisdom exists because it corresponds to a possibility, that of the human manifestation of the Divine Science.

"For she is the breath of the power of God, and a pure influence flowing from the glory of the Almighty: therefore can no defiled thing fall into her. . . . After the light cometh night: but vice shall not prevail against wisdom."

Concerning Forms in Art

1

It may seem surprising that we should introduce a subject that not only appears to have little or no connection with anything that has gone before, but also in itself seems to be of secondary importance; in fact, however, this question of forms in art is by no means a negligible one and is closely connected with the general questions dealt with in this book.

First of all, however, there is a matter of terminology that calls for a few words of explanation: in speaking of "forms in art" and not just "forms," our purpose is to make it clear that we are not dealing with abstract forms, but on the contrary, with things that are sensible by definition; if on the other hand, we avoid speaking of "artistic forms," it is because the epithet "artistic" carries with it, in present-day language, a notion of luxury and therefore of superfluity, and this corresponds to something diametrically opposed to what we have in mind. The expression "forms in art" is really a pleonasm, inasmuch as it is not possible, traditionally speaking, to dissociate form from art, the latter being simply the principle of manifestation of the former; however, we have been obliged to use this pleonasm for the reasons just given.

If the importance of forms is to be understood, it is necessary to appreciate the fact that it is the sensible form that, symbolically, corresponds most directly to the Intellect, by reason of the inverse analogy connecting the principial and manifested orders.* In consequence of this analogy the highest realities are most clearly manifested in their remotest reflections, namely, in the sensible or material order, and herein lies the deepest meaning of the proverb "Extremes meet"; to which one might add that it is for this same reason that Revelation descended not only into the souls of the Prophets, but also into their bodies, which presupposed their physical perfection.† Sensible forms therefore correspond with exactness to intellections, and it is for this reason that traditional art has rules that apply the cosmic laws and universal principles to the domain of forms, and that, beneath their more general outward aspect, reveal the style of the civilization under consideration, this style in its turn rendering explicit the form of intellectuality of that civilization. When art ceases to be traditional and becomes human, individual, and therefore arbitrary, that is infallibly the sign—and secondarily the cause—of an intellectual decline, a weakening, which, in the sight of those who are skilled in the "discernment of spirits" and who look upon things with an unprejudiced eye, is expressed by the more or less incoherent and spiritually insignificant, we would go even as far as to say unintelligible character of the forms.‡ In order to forestall any possible objection, we would

---

* "Art," said St. Thomas Aquinas, "is associated with knowledge."

† René Guénon ("Les deux nuits," *Études Traditionnelles,* April and May, 1939) in speaking of the *laylat al-qadr,* night of the "descent" (*tanzīl*) of the Koran, points out that

this night, according to Muhyi 'd-Dīn ibn 'Arabī's commentary, is identified with the actual body of the Prophet. What is particularly important to note is the fact that the "revelation" is received, not in the mind, but in the body of the being who is commissioned to express the Principle. "And the Word was made flesh," says the Gospel ("flesh" and not "mind") and this is but another way of expressing, under the form proper to the Christian Tradition, the reality that is represented by the *laylat al-qadr* in the Islamic Tradition.

This truth is closely bound up with the relationship mentioned as existing between forms and intellections.

‡ We are referring here to the decadence of certain branches of religious art during the Gothic period, especially in its latter part, and to Western art as a whole from the Renaissance onward: Christian art (architecture, sculpture, painting, liturgical goldsmithery, and so on), which formerly was sacred, symbolical, and spiritual, had to give way before the invasion of neo-antique and naturalistic, individualistic, and sentimental art; this art, which contained absolutely nothing "miraculous"—no matter what those who be-

stress the fact that in intellectually healthy civilizations—the Christian civilization of the Middle Ages, for instance—spirituality often affirms itself by a marked indifference to forms, and sometimes even reveals a tendency to turn away from them, as is shown by the example of St. Bernard when he condemned images in monasteries, which, it must be said, in nowise signifies the acceptance of ugliness and barbarism, any more than poverty implies the possession of things that are mean in themselves. But in a world where traditional art is dead, where consequently form itself is invaded by everything that is contrary to spirituality and where nearly every formal expression is corrupted at its very roots, the traditional regularity of forms takes on a very special spiritual importance that it could not have possessed at the beginning, since the absence of the spirit in forms was then inconceivable.

What has been said concerning the intellectual quality of sensible forms must not make us overlook the fact that the further one goes back to the origins of a given religion, the less those forms appear in a state of full development. The pseudoform, that is to say, an arbitrary form, is always excluded, as already stated, but form as such can also be virtually absent, at least in certain more or less peripheral domains. On the other hand, the nearer one draws to the end of the religious cycle under consideration, the greater the importance attaching to formalism, even from the so-called artistic point of view, since the forms have by

---

lieve in the "Greek miracle" may care to think—is quite unfitted for the transmission of intellectual intuitions and no longer answers to anything higher than collective psychic aspirations; it is thus as far removed as can be from intellectual contemplation and takes into consideration sentimentality only; moreover, sentimentality debases itself in the measure that it caters to the needs of the masses, until it ends in a saccharine and bathetic vulgarity. It is strange that no one has understood to what a degree this barbarism of forms, which reached a zenith of empty and miserable exhibitionism in the period of Louis XV, contributed—and still contributes—to driving many souls (and by no means the worst) away from the Church; they feel literally choked in surroundings that do not allow their intelligence room to breathe. Let us note in passing that the historical connection between the new St. Peter's Basilica in Rome—of the Renaissance period, therefore antispiritual and showy, "human" one might say—and the origin of the Reformation are unfortunately very far from fortuitous.

then become almost indispensable channels for the actualization of the spiritual deposit of the religion.* What should never be forgotten is the fact that the absence of the formal element is not equivalent to the presence of the amorphous, and vice versa; the amorphous and the barbarous will never attain the majestic beauty of the void, whatever may be believed by those who have an interest in passing off a deficiency for a superiority.† This law of compensation, by virtue of which certain relationships of proportion undergo a more or less marked inversion during the course of a religious cycle, can be applied in all spheres: for instance, we may quote the following saying (*ḥadīth*) of the Prophet Mohammed: "In the beginning of Islam, he who omits a tenth of the Law

* This point is one that is ignored by certain pseudo-Hindu movements, whether of Indian origin or not, which move away from the sacred forms of Hinduism while believing themselves to represent its purest essence; in reality it is useless to confer a spiritual means on a man without having first of all forged in him a mentality that will be in harmony with this means, and that quite independently of the obligation of a personal attachment to an initiatory line; a spiritual realization is inconceivable outside the appropriate psychic climate, that is to say, one that is in conformity with the religious ambiance of the spiritual means in question. We may perhaps be allowed to add a remark here that seems to take us rather outside our subject, though some readers, at least, will understand its appropriateness: an objection might be raised to what we have just been saying on the grounds that Shrī Chaitanya bestowed initiation not only on Hindus but on Moslems as well; this objection, however, is pointless in the present case, for what Shrī Chaitanya, who was one of the greatest spiritual Masters of India, transmitted first and foremost was a current of grace resulting from the intense radiation of his own holiness; this radiation had the virtue of in some degree obliterating or drowning formal differences, which is all the more admissible in that he was "bhaktic" by nature. Besides, the fact that Shrī Chaitanya could accomplish miracles in nowise implies that another guru, even if he were of the same initiatory lineage and therefore a legitimate successor of Chaitanya, could do the same; from another point of view that, though less important, is by no means negligible, one must also take into consideration the psychic and other affinities that may exist between Hindu and Moslem Indians, especially in the case of contemplatives, so that formal divergences can a priori be greatly attenuated in certain cases.

† The claim has sometimes been put forward that Christianity, on the ground that it stands above forms, cannot be identified with any particular civilization; it is indeed understandable that some people would like to find consolation for the loss of Christian civilization, including its art, but the opinion we have just quoted is nonetheless inexcusable.

is damned; but in the latter days, he who shall accomplish a tenth thereof will be saved."

The analogical relationship between intellections and material forms explains how it became possible for esoterism to be grafted onto the exercise of the crafts and especially architectural art; the cathedrals that the Christian initiates left behind them offer the most explicit as well as the most dazzling proof of the spiritual exaltation of the Middle Ages.* This brings us to a most important aspect of the question now before us, namely, the action of esoterism on exoterism through the medium of sensible forms, the production of which is precisely the prerogative of craft initiation. Through these forms, which act as vehicles of the integral religious doctrine, and which thanks to their symbolism translate this doctrine into a language that is both immediate and universal, esoterism infuses an intellectual quality into the properly devotional part of the tradition, thereby establishing a balance the absence of which would finally bring about the dissolution of the whole civilization, as has happened in the Christian world. The abandoning of sacred art deprived esoterism of its most direct means of action; the outward religion insisted more and more on its own peculiarities, that is to say, its limitations, until finally, by want of that current of universality that, through the language of forms, had quickened and stabilized the religious civilization, reactions in a contrary sense were brought about; that is to say, the formal limitations, instead of being compensated and thereby stabilized by means of the supraformal interferences of esoterism, gave rise, through their opacity or massiveness, to negations that might be qualified as infraformal, resulting as they did from an individual arbitrariness that, far from being a form of the truth, was merely a formless chaos of opinions and fancies.

To return to our initial idea, it may be added that the Beauty of God corresponds to a deeper reality than His Goodness, no matter how paradoxical this may appear at first sight. One has only to recall the metaphysical law in virtue of which the analogy between

* When standing before a cathedral, a person really feels he is placed at the center of the world; standing before a church of the Renaissance, Baroque, or Rococo periods, he merely feels himself to be in Europe.

the principial and manifested orders is reversed, in the sense that what is principially great will be small in the manifested order and that which is inward in the Principle will appear as outward in manifestation, and vice versa. It is because of this inverse analogy that in man beauty is outward and goodness inward—at least in the usual sense of these words—contrary to what obtains in the principial order where Goodness is itself an expression of Beauty.

2

It has often been noticed that Oriental peoples, including those reputed to be the most artistic, show themselves for the most part entirely lacking in aesthetic discernment with regard to whatever comes to them from the West. All the ugliness born of a world more and more devoid of spirituality spreads over the East with unbelievable facility, not only under the influence of politico-economic factors, which would not be so surprising, but also by the free consent of those who, by all appearances, had created a world of beauty, that is, a civilization, in which every expression, including the most modest, bore the imprint of the same genius. Since the very beginning of Western infiltration, it has been astonishing to see the most perfect works of art set side by side with the worst trivialities of industrial production, and these disconcerting contradictions have taken place not only in the realm of objects of art, but in nearly every sphere, setting aside the fact that in a normal civilization everything accomplished by man is related to the domain of art, in some respects at least. The answer to this paradox is very simple, however, and we have already outlined it in the preceding pages: it resides in the fact that forms, even the most unimportant, are the work of human hands in a secondary manner only; they originate first and foremost from the same suprahuman source from which all tradition originates, which is another way of saying that the artist who lives in a traditional world without fissures works under the discipline or the inspiration of a genius that surpasses him; fundamentally he is but the instrument of this genius, if only from the fact of his craftsman's qualification.* Consequently individual taste plays only a relatively subordinate part in the production of the forms of such an art, and this taste will be reduced to nothing as soon as the individual finds himself face to face with a form that is foreign to the spirit of his own religion; that is what happens in the case of a people unfamiliar with Western civilization when they encounter the forms imported from the West. However, for this to happen it is necessary that the people accepting such confusion should no longer be fully conscious of their own spiritual genius, or in other terms, that they should no longer be capable of understanding the forms with which they are still surrounded and in which they live; it is in fact a proof that the people in question are already suffering from a certain decadence. Because of this fact, they are led to accept modern ugliness all the more easily because it may answer to certain inferior possibilities that those people are already spontaneously seeking to realize, no matter how, and it may

* A thing is not only what it is for the senses, but also what it represents. Natural or artificial objects are not . . . arbitrary "symbols" of such or such a different or superior reality; but they are . . . the effective manifestation of that reality: the eagle or the lion, for example, is not so much the symbol or the image of the Sun as it *is* the Sun under one of its manifestations (the essential form being more important than the nature in which it manifests itself); in the same way, every house is the world in effigy and every altar is situated at the centre of the earth. . . . [Ananda K. Coomaraswamy, "The Primitive Mentality," *Études Traditionnelles,* August-September-October, 1939]

It is solely and exclusively traditional art—in the widest sense of the word, implying all that is of an externally formal order, and therefore *a fortiori* everything that belongs in some way or other to the ritual domain —it is only this art, transmitted with tradition and by tradition, that can guarantee the adequate analogical correspondence between the Divine and the cosmic orders, on the one hand, and the human or artistic order, on the other. As a result, the traditional artist does not limit himself simply to imitating Nature, but to "imitating Nature in her manner of operation" (Thomas Aquinas, *Sum. Theol.* I, qu. 117, a. I), and it goes without saying that the artist cannot, with his own individual means, improvise such a cosmological operation. It is by the entirely adequate conformity of the artist to this "manner of operation," a conformity that is subordinated to the rules of tradition, that the masterpiece is created; in other words, this conformity essentially presupposes a knowledge, which may be either personal, direct, and active, or inherited, indirect, and passive, the latter case being that of those artisans who, unconscious as individuals of the metaphysical content of the forms they have learned to create, know not how to resist the corrosive influence of the modern West.

well be quite subconsciously; therefore, the unreasoning readiness
with which only too many Orientals (possibly even the great majority) accept things that are utterly incompatible with the spirit of
their religion is best explained by the fascination exercised over
the ordinary man by something corresponding to an as yet unex-
hausted possibility, this possibility being, in the present case, simply
that of arbitrariness or want of principle. However that may be, and
without wishing to attach too much importance to this explanation
of what appears to be the complete lack of taste shown by Orientals,
there is one fact that is absolutely certain, namely, that very many
Orientals themselves no longer understand the sense of the forms
they have inherited from their ancestors, together with their whole
religion. All that has just been said applies of course first and
foremost and *a fortiori* to the nations of the West themselves, who,
after having created—we will not say "invented"—a perfect traditional art, proceeded to disown it in favor of the residues of the
individualistic and empty art of the Graeco-Romans, which has
finally led to the artistic chaos of the modern world. We know
very well that there are some who will not at any price admit the
unintelligibility or the ugliness of the modern world, and who
readily employ the word "aesthetic," with a derogatory nuance
similar to that attaching to the words "picturesque" and "romantic," in order to discredit in advance the importance of forms so
that they may find themselves more at ease in the enclosed system
of their own barbarism. Such an attitude has nothing surprising in
it when it concerns avowed modernists, but it is worse than illog-
ical, not to say rather despicable, coming from those who claim to
belong to the Christian civilization; for to reduce the spontaneous
and normal language of Christian art—a language the beauty of
which can hardly be questioned—to a worldly matter of taste—
as if medieval art could have been the product of mere caprice—
amounts to admitting that the imprint given by the genius of Christianity to all its direct and indirect expressions was only a contingency unrelated to that genius and devoid of serious importance,
or even due to a mental inferiority; for "only the spirit matters"—
so say certain ignorant people imbued with hypocritical, icono-
clastic, blasphemous, and impotent puritanism, who pronounce

the word "spirit" all the more readily because they are the last to know what it really stands for.

In order to understand the causes of the decadence of art in the West, one must take into account the fact that there is in the European mentality a certain dangerous idealism that is not without relevance to that decadence, nor yet to the decay of Western civilization as a whole. This idealism has found its fullest, one might say its most intelligent, expression in certain forms of Gothic art, those in which a kind of dynamism is predominant, which seems to aim at taking away the heaviness from stone. As for Byzantine and Romanesque art, as well as that other side of Gothic art wherein a static power has been preserved, it might be said that it is an essentially intellectual art, therefore realistic. The flamboyant Gothic art, no matter how "passionate" it became, was nevertheless still a traditional art except in the case of sculpture and painting, which were already well on the way to decadence; to be more exact, it was the "swan song" of Gothic art. From the time of the Renaissance, which represents a sort of posthumous revenge on the part of classical antiquity, European idealism flowed into the exhumed sarcophagi of the Graeco-Roman civilization. By this act of suicide, it placed itself at the service of an individualism in which it thought to have rediscovered its own genius, only to end up, after a number of intermediate stages, in the grossest and most fantastic affirmations of that individualism. This was really a double suicide: firstly, the forsaking of medieval or Christian art, and secondly, the adoption of Graeco-Roman forms that intoxicated the Christian world with the poison of their decadence. But it is necessary here to consider a possible objection: was not the art of the first Christians in fact Roman art? The answer is that the real beginnings of Christian art are to be found in the symbols inscribed in the catacombs, and not in the forms that the early Christians, themselves in part belonging to the Roman civilization, temporarily borrowed in a purely outward manner from the classical decadence. Christianity was indeed called upon to replace this decadence by an art springing spontaneously from an original spiritual genius, and if in fact certain Roman influences have always persisted in Christian art, this only applies to more or less superficial details.

It has just been stated that European idealism allied itself to individualism and ended by identifying itself with the crudest expressions of the latter. As for those things that the West finds "crude" in other civilizations, they are nearly always only the more or less superficial aspects of a realism that scorns delusive and hypocritical veils. However, one should not lose sight of the fact that idealism is not bad in itself, inasmuch as it finds its place in the mentality of heroes, always inclined toward sublimation; what is bad, and at the same time specifically Western, is the intrusion of this mentality into every sphere, including those in which it has no place. It is this distorted idealism, all the more fragile and dangerous because it is distorted, that Islam, with its desire for equilibrium and stability—in other words, realism—wished to avoid at all costs, having, moreover, taken into consideration the restricted possibilities of the present cyclic period, already far removed from its origin; herein lies the reason for that "earthy" aspect with which Christians are wont to reproach the Islamic civilization.

3

In order to give an idea of the principles of traditional art, we will point out a few of the most general and elementary ones: first of all, the work executed must conform to the use to which it will be put, and it must express that conformity; if there be an added symbolism, it must conform to the symbolism inherent in the object; there must be no conflict between the essential and the accessory, but a hierarchical harmony, which will moreover spring from the purity of the symbolism; the treatment of the material used must be in conformity with the nature of that material in the same way that the material itself must be in conformity with the use of the object; lastly, the object must not give an illusion of being other than what it really is, for such an illusion always gives a disagreeable impression of uselessness, and when this illusion is the goal of the finished work, as it is in the case of all classicist art, it is the mark of a uselessness that is only too apparent. The great innovations of naturalistic art can be reduced in fact to so many violations of the principles of normal art: firstly, as far as sculpture is concerned, violation of the inert material used, whether it be stone, metal, or wood; and secondly, in the case of painting, violation of the plane surface. In the first example, the inert material is treated as if it were endowed with life, whereas it is essentially static and only allows, because of this fact, the representation either of motionless bodies or of essential or schematic phases of movement, but not that of arbitrary, accidental, or as it were, fragmentary movements; in the second example, that of painting, the plane surface is treated as if it had three dimensions, both by means of foreshortening and by the use of shadows.

It will be appreciated that rules such as these are not dictated by merely aesthetic reasons, and that they represent, on the contrary, applications of cosmic and Divine laws; beauty will flow from them as a necessary result. As regards beauty in naturalistic art, it does not reside in the work as such, but solely in the object that it copies, whereas in symbolic and traditional art it is the work in itself that is beautiful, whether it be abstract or whether it borrow beauty in a greater or lesser degree from a natural model. It would be difficult to find a better illustration of this distinction than that afforded by a comparison between so-called classical Greek art and Egyptian art: the beauty of the latter does not, in fact, lie simply and solely in the object represented, but resides simultaneously and *a fortiori* in the work as such, that is to say, in the inward reality that the work makes manifest. The fact that naturalistic art has sometimes succeeded in expressing nobility of feeling or vigorous intelligence is not in question and may be explained by cosmological reasons that could not but exist; but that has no connection with art as such, and no individual value could ever make up for the falsification of the latter.

The majority of moderns who claim to understand art are convinced that Byzantine or Romanesque art is in no way superior to modern art, and that a Byzantine or Romanesque Virgin resembles Mary no more than do her naturalistic images, in fact rather the contrary. The answer is, however, quite simple: the Byzantine Virgin—which traditionally goes back to Saint Luke and the Angels—is infinitely closer to the truth of Mary than a naturalistic image, which of necessity is always that of another woman. Only one of two things is possible: either the artist presents an absolutely correct portrait of the Virgin from a physical point of view, in which case it will be necessary for the artist to have seen the Virgin, a condition that cannot easily be fulfilled—setting aside the fact that all purely naturalistic painting is illegitimate—or else the artist will present a perfectly adequate symbol of the Virgin, but in this case physical resemblance, without being absolutely excluded, is no longer at all in question. It is this second solution that is realized in icons; what they do not express by means of a physical resemblance they express by the abstract but immediate language of symbolism, a language that is built up of precision and imponderables both together. Thus the icon, in addition to the beatific power that is inherent in it by reason of its sacramental character, transmits the holiness or inner reality of the Virgin and hence the universal reality of which the Virgin herself is an expression; in suggesting both a contemplative experience and a metaphysical truth, the icon becomes a support of intellection, whereas a naturalistic image transmits—apart from its obvious and inevitable falsehood—only the fact that Mary was a woman. It is true that in the case of a particular icon, it may happen that the proportions and features are those of the living Virgin, but such a likeness, if it really came to pass, would be independent of the symbolism of the image and could only be the result of a special inspiration. Naturalistic art could moreover be legitimate up to a certain point if it were used exclusively to record the features of the saints, since the contemplation of saints (the Hindu *darshan*) can be a very precious help in the spiritual way, owing to the fact that their outward appearance conveys, as it were, the perfume of their spirituality; but the use in this limited manner of a partial and disciplined naturalism corresponds only to a very remote possibility.

To come back to the symbolic and spiritual quality of the icon: one's ability to perceive the spiritual quality of an icon or any other symbol is a question of contemplative intelligence and also of "sacred science." However, it is certainly false to claim, in justification of naturalism, that the people need an accessible, that is to say, a platitudinous, art, for it is not the people who gave birth to the Renaissance; the art of the latter, like all the "fine art" that is derived from it, is, on the contrary, an offense to the piety of the simple person. The artistic ideals of the Renaissance and of all modern art are therefore very far removed from what the people need, and in fact nearly all the miraculous Virgins to which the people flock are Byzantine or Romanesque; and who would presume to argue that the black coloring of some of them agrees with popular taste or is particularly accessible to it? On the other hand, the Virgins made by the hands of the people, when they have not been corrupted by the influence of academic art, are very much "truer," even if it be only in a subjective way, than those of the latter; and even if one were prepared to admit that the majority demand images that are shallow and silly, can it be said that the needs of the elite have no right to existence?

In the preceding paragraphs we have already implicitly answered the question as to whether sacred art is meant to cater for the intellectual elite alone, or whether it has something to offer to the man of average intelligence. This question solves itself when one takes into consideration the universality of all symbolism, for this universality enables sacred art to transmit—apart from metaphysical truths and facts derived from sacred history—not only spiritual states, but psychological attitudes that are accessible to all men; in modern parlance, one might say that such art is both profound and naïve at the same time, and this combination of profundity and naïveté is precisely one of the dominant characteristics of sacred art. The ingenuousness or candor of such art, far from being due to a spontaneous or affected inferiority, reveals, on the contrary, the normal state of the human soul, whether it be that of the average or of the superior man; the apparent intelligence of naturalism, on the other hand, that is to say, its well-nigh satanic skill in copying Nature and thus transmitting nothing but the hollow shell of beings and things, can only correspond to a deformed mentality, we might say to one that has deviated from primordial simplicity or innocence. It goes without saying that such a deformation, resulting as it does from intellectual superficiality and mental virtuosity, is incompatible with the traditional spirit and consequently finds no place in a civilization that has remained faithful to that spirit. Therefore if sacred art appeals to contemplative intelligence, it likewise appeals to normal human sensibility. This means that such art alone possesses a universal language, and that none is better fitted to appeal, not only to an elite, but also to the people at large. Let us remember, too, as far as the apparently childlike aspect of the traditional mentality is concerned, Christ's injunction to be "as little children" and "simple as doves," words that, no matter what may be their spiritual meaning, also quite plainly refer to psychological realities.

The Fathers of the eighth century, very different from those religious authorities of the fifteenth and sixteenth centuries who betrayed Christian art by abandoning it to the impure passions of worldly men and the ignorant imagination of the profane, were fully conscious of the holiness of all the means of expression belonging to their religion. They stipulated, at the second council of Nicaea, that "art [the integral perfection of work] alone belongs to the painter, while ordinance [the choice of the subject] and disposition [the treatment of the subject from the symbolical as well as the technical or material points of view] belongs to the Fathers" (*Non est pictoris—ejus enim sola ars est—verum ordinatio et dispositio Patrum nostrorum*). This amounts to placing all artistic initiative under the direct and active authority of the spiritual leaders of Christianity. Such being the case, how can one explain the fact that during recent centuries religious circles have, for the most part, shown such a regrettable lack of understanding regarding all those things that, having an artistic character, are, in their opinion, only external matters? First of all, admitting a priori the elimination of esoteric influence, there is the fact that a religious perspective as such has a tendency to identify itself with the moral point of view, which stresses merit only and believes it is necessary to ignore the sanctifying quality of intellectual knowledge and, as a result, the value of the supports of such knowledge; now, the perfection of sensible forms is no more meritorious in the moral sense than the intellections that those forms reflect and transmit, and it is therefore only logical that symbolic forms, when they are no longer understood, should be relegated to the background, and even forsaken, in order to be replaced by forms that will no longer appeal to the intelligence, but only to a sentimental imagination capable of inspiring the meritorious act—at least such is the belief of the man of limited intelligence. However, this sort of speculative provocation of reactions by resorting to means of a superficial and vulgar nature will, in the last analysis, prove to be illusory, for, in reality, nothing can be better fitted to influence the deeper dispositions of the soul than sacred art. Profane art, on the contrary, even if it be of some psychological value in the case of souls of inferior intelligence, soon exhausts its means, by the very fact of their superficiality and vulgarity, after which it can only provoke reactions of contempt; these are only too common, and may be considered as a rebound of the contempt in which sacred art was held by profane art, especially in its earlier stages.* It has been a matter of current experience that nothing is able to offer to irreligion a more immediately tangible nourishment than the insipid hypocrisy of religious images; that which was meant to stimulate piety in the believer but serves to confirm unbelievers in their impiety, whereas it must be recognized that genuinely sacred art does not possess this character of a "two-edged sword," for being itself more abstract, it offers much less hold to hostile psychological reactions. Now, no matter what may be the theories that attribute to the people the need for an unintelligent and radically falsified imagery, the elite does exist and certainly needs something different; what it requires is an art that evokes, not human platitudes, but Divine depths. Such a language cannot spring simply from profane taste, nor even from genius, but must proceed essentially out of religion—which demands that the work of art be executed by an artist who is saintly, or at least "in a state of grace."† Far from serving only for the more or less super-

---

* In the same way, the hostility of the representatives of exoterism for all that lies beyond their comprehension results in an increasingly massive exoterism that cannot but suffer from fissures; but the spiritual "porousness" of religion—that is to say, the immanence in the substance of exoterism of a transcendent dimension that makes up for its massiveness—this state of porousness having been lost, the above-mentioned fissures could be produced only from below, which means in fact the replacement of the Masters of medieval esoterism by the protagonists of modern unbelief.

† The icon painters were monks who, before setting to work, prepared themselves by fasting, prayer, confession, and communion; it even happened

ficial instruction and edification of the masses, the icon, as is the case with the Hindu *yantra* and all other visible symbols, establishes a bridge from the sensible to the spiritual: "By the visible aspect," states St. John Damascene, "our thoughts must be drawn up in a spiritual flight and rise to the invisible majesty of God."

But let us return to the errors of naturalism. Art, as soon as it is no longer determined, illuminated, and guided by spirituality, lies at the mercy of the individual and purely psychic resources of the artist, and these resources must soon run out, if only because of the very platitude of the naturalistic principle that calls only for a superficial copying of Nature. Reaching the extreme limit of its own platitude, naturalism inevitably engendered the monstrosities of surrealism. The latter is but the decomposing body of an art and, in any case, should rather be called "infrarealism"; it is, properly speaking, the satanic consequence of naturalistic luciferianism. Naturalism, as a matter of fact, is clearly luciferian in its wish to imitate the creations of God, not to mention its affirmation of the psychic element to the detriment of the spiritual, or of the individual to the detriment of the universal, and above all, of the bare fact to the detriment of the symbol. Normally man must imitate the creative act, not the thing created; that is what is done by symbolic art, and the results are "creations" that are not would-be duplications of those of God, but rather a reflection of them according to a real analogy, revealing the transcendental aspects of things; and this revelation is the only sufficient reason of art, apart from the practical usefulness of its objects. There is here a metaphysical inversion of relation that we have already pointed out: for God, His creature reflects an exteriorized aspect of Himself; for the artist, on the contrary, the work is a reflection of an inner reality of which he himself is only an outward aspect; God creates His own image, while man, so to speak, fashions his own essence, at least symbolically. On the principial plane, the inner manifests itself in the outer, but on the manifested plane, the outer fashions the inner,

---

that the colors were mixed with holy water and the dust from relics, as would not have been possible had the icon not possessed a truly sacramental character.

and a sufficient reason for all traditional art, no matter of what kind, is the fact that in a certain sense the work is greater than the artist himself, and brings back the latter, through the mystery of artistic creation, to the proximity of his own Divine Essence.*

* This explains the danger, so far as Semitic peoples are concerned, that lies in the painting and especially in the carving of living beings. Where the Hindu or the East Asian adores a Divine reality through a symbol—and it is to be remembered that a symbol is truly what it symbolizes as far as its essential reality is concerned—the Semite will display a tendency to deify the symbol itself; one of the reasons for the prohibition of plastic and pictorial arts amongst the Semitic peoples is certainly the intention to prevent naturalistic deviations, a very real danger among men whose mentality is predominantly individualistic and sentimental.

Limits of Religious Expansion

1

We must now return to the more direct aspects of the question of the unity of religious forms, and we propose to show in this chapter how the symbolic universality of each of these forms implies limitations in relation to universality in the absolute sense. True affirmations, being concerned with sacred facts—such as, for example, the person of Christ—that necessarily and by definition manifest universal truths, are liable to become false to a greater or lesser degree when artificially removed from their providential framework. So far as Christianity is concerned, this framework is the Western world, in which Christ is "the Life," with the definite article and without epithet. Modern disorder has destroyed this framework and humanity has outwardly expanded in an artificial or quantitative manner. As a result, some people refuse to admit other "Christs," while others arrive at the opposite conclusion and deny to Jesus the quality of Christ. It is as though certain persons, when faced with the discovery of other solar systems, continued to maintain the view that there is only one sun, our own, whereas others, perceiving that our sun is not the only one, denied that it was a sun and concluded that there was no such thing, since none was unique. The truth of the matter lies between the two opinions: our sun truly is "the sun," but it is unique solely in relation to the system of which it is the center; just as there are many solar systems, so there are many suns, but this does not prevent each being unique by definition. The sun, the lion, the eagle, the sunflower, honey, amber, gold, are so many natural manifestations of the solar principle, each unique and symbolically absolute in its own domain; the fact that they cease to be unique when detached from the limits that enclose these domains and make of them so many closed systems or microcosms, the relativity of their unicity being then revealed, is in no way inconsistent with the fact that, within their respective domains and for these domains, these manifestations are really identified with the solar principle, clothing it in modes appropriate to the possibilities of the domain they belong to. To state that Christ is not "the Son of God," but only "a Son of God," would thus be false, for the Word is unique and each of its manifestations essentially reflects this Divine unicity.

Certain passages of the New Testament contain indications that the "world" in which Christ is "the Sun" is identified with the Roman Empire, which represented the providential sphere of expansion and life for the Christian civilization. When mention is made in these texts of "every nation under heaven" (Acts 2:5–11), it is in fact only nations known to the Roman world that are referred to;[1] and similarly, when it is said there is "none other name under heaven given among men whereby we must be saved" (Acts 4:12), there is no reason to suppose that the expression "under heaven" means anything more than it does in the first-mentioned passage; unless, of course, the name "Jesus" be understood as a symbolic designation of the Word Itself, which would imply that in the world there is one name only, the Word, by which men can be saved, whatever the Divine manifestation designated by this name in any particular case, or in other words, whatever the particular form of this eternal Name, be it "Jesus," "Buddha," or any other.

This raises a question that cannot be passed over in silence, namely, whether the activity of missionaries working outside the predestined and normal world of Christianity is altogether illegitimate. To this it must be answered that missionaries—although they have profited from abnormal circumstances inasmuch as Western expansion at the expense of other civilizations is due solely to a crushing material superiority arising out of the modern deviation—follow a way that possesses, at least in principle, a sacrificial aspect; consequently the subjective reality of this way will always retain its mystic meaning, independent of the objective reality of missionary activity. The positive aspect that this activity derives from its evangelical origin cannot in fact entirely be lost merely through overstepping the boundaries of the Christian world—which indeed had been done before modern times, though in exceptional circumstances and under quite different conditions—and by encroaching upon worlds that, though not having the Christ Jesus, are "Christian" inasmuch as they have the Universal Christ who is the Word that inspires all Revelation, and therefore do not need conversion. But this positive aspect of missionary activity is only manifested in the objective world in more or less exceptional cases, as when the spiritual influence emanating from a saint or relic proves stronger than the force of an autochthonous spiritual influence weakened by the existing materialism of the local environment, or because Christianity is better suited to the particular mentality of certain individuals, which necessarily supposes a lack of comprehension by the latter of their own religion, and the presence in them of aspirations, spiritual or otherwise, that Christianity under one form or another will satisfy. Most of these remarks are of course also applicable in an inverse sense and in favor of non-Christian religions, with the difference, however, that in this case conversions are much more rare, for reasons not complimentary to the West. In the first place, the East possesses no colonies or "protectorates" in the West and does not maintain powerfully protected missions there; and secondly, Westerners turn much more readily to pure and simple unbelief than to an alien spirituality.* As for the reservations that can be made in regard to. missionary activity, it is important never to lose sight of the fact that they cannot concern its direct and evangelical aspect—except as regards the inevitable diminution and even the decadence of this aspect itself, due to the abnormal circumstances already referred

* Since the middle of the twentieth century, however, we have witnessed the phenomenon of an increasing number of Westerners turning to forms of Oriental spirituality, authentic or false.

to—but simply and solely its active solidarity with modern Western barbarism.

We will take this opportunity of pointing out that the East was already in a state of great decadence at the time when Western expansion began, though this decadence can by no means be compared with the decadence of the modern West, the nature of which is, in certain secondary respects at least, the very reverse of that of Eastern decadence. Whereas the latter is passive and may be compared to the decay of a physical organism worn out with age, the specifically modern decadence is, on the contrary, active and voluntary, cerebral, so to speak, and it is this that gives to the Westerner the illusion of a superiority that, even if it really exists on a certain psychological plane by reason of the difference we have just mentioned, is nonetheless very relative and disappears altogether when contrasted with the spiritual superiority of the East. It could also be said that the decadence of the East is based on inertia, while that of the West is based on error; the only thing that links the two together is the common predominance of the passional element, and it is in fact the predominance of this element that, in the human sphere, characterizes the Dark Age in which the whole world is immersed and that was foretold by all the sacred doctrines. If this difference in the modes of decadence explains, on the one hand, the contempt that many Westerners experience on meeting certain Orientals—a contempt that unfortunately is not always the result of mere prejudice as is the case where hatred of the traditional East is concerned—and on the other, the blind admiration that too many Orientals have for certain positive elements in the Western mentality, it also goes without saying that the contempt of the old East for the modern West is justified in a way that is not merely psychological, and therefore relative and debatable, but on the contrary complete and total, because it is founded on spiritual reasons that alone are decisive. In the eyes of the East when faithful to its own spirit, the "progress" of Westerners will never be anything but a vicious circle that vainly seeks to eliminate inevitable miseries at the cost of the only thing that gives any meaning to life.

But let us return once more to the missionary question. The fact that it may be legitimate to pass from one religious form to another in no way prevents a real apostasy in certain cases: an apostate is one who changes from one religious form to another without valid reason; on the other hand, when a conversion takes place from one orthodox religion to another, the reasons invoked have at least a subjective validity. It goes without saying that it is possible to pass from one religious form to another without being converted, which may happen for reasons of esoteric, and therefore spiritual, expediency; in this case, the reasons determining such a passage will be objectively as well as subjectivly valid, or rather it will no longer be possible to speak of subjective reasons in any sense.

We have already seen that the attitude of exoterism relative to alien religious forms is determined by two factors, one positive and the other negative, the first being the character of unicity inherent in every Revelation, and the second, which is an extrinsic consequence of this unicity, the rejection of a particular "paganism." So far as Christianity is concerned, it is sufficient to situate it within its normal limits of expansion—which, apart from rare exceptions, it would never have overstepped but for the modern deviation—to understand that these two factors are not literally applicable outside their quasi-natural limits, but have, on the contrary, to be universalized, that is to say, transposed onto the plane of the Primordial Tradition that lives perpetually in every orthodox religious form. In other words, it is necessary to understand that each of these alien religious forms can also lay claim to this unicity and this right to deny "paganism," which amounts to saying that each one, by its intrinsic orthodoxy, is a form of what in Christian language is called the "Eternal Church."

It cannot be too strongly emphasized that the literal meaning of the Divine sayings concerning human contingencies is by definition a limited meaning; that is to say, it stops short at the confines of the particular realm to which it is destined to apply in accordance with the Divine intention—the criterion of which resides fundamentally in the very nature of things, at least under normal conditions—and it is the purely spiritual meaning alone that is able to lay claim to absoluteness. The injunction to "teach all nations" is no exception, any more than are other sayings where the natural limitation of their literal meaning is obvious to everyone, doubtless because there is no advantage to be gained by conferring an unconditional meaning upon them: examples that come to mind are the commandment against killing, or the instruction to turn the left cheek, or that against using vain repetitions in prayer, and finally the command to take no thought for the morrow. Nevertheless, the Divine Master never specified in so many words the limits within which these injunctions were valid, so that logically their bearing might be considered to be unconditional, as it is in the case of the injunction to "teach all nations." That being said, it is nevertheless important to add that the directly literal meaning, the word-for-word interpretation, is obviously included also to a certain degree, not only in the command to preach to all nations, but also in the other sayings of Christ we have just mentioned; what matters is to be able to put this meaning in its proper place, without excluding other possible meanings. If it be true that the command to teach all nations cannot be read as being absolutely limited in its purpose to the establishment of the Christian world, but also implies, in a secondary way, the preaching of the Gospel to all peoples within reach, it is quite as true that the injunction to turn the left cheek is also to be understood literally in certain cases of spiritual discipline; but it also follows that the latter interpretation will be just as secondary as the literal interpretation of the command to preach to all peoples. In order to define clearly the difference between the primary meaning of this command and its secondary meaning, we will recall the distinction already drawn earlier on, namely, that in the first case the end is primarily objective, since it is a question of establishing the Christian world, while in the second case, that of preaching to people of alien civilizations, the end is primarily subjective and spiritual, in the sense that its inward aspect is more important than its outward one, which here is only a support for sacrificial realization. By way of objection the following words of Christ may no doubt be quoted: "This Gospel of the Kingdom will be taught among all men, as a testimony to all nations; then the end will come"; but the answer is that if these words refer to the whole world and not just to the West, it is because they are not a command but a prophecy, and because they relate to cyclic conditions in which separating barriers between the different traditional worlds will have disappeared; in other words, we can say that "Christ," who for the Hindus will be the Kalki *Avatāra* and for the Buddhists the *Bodhisattva* Maitreya, will restore the Primordial Tradition.

2

We have said above that the commandment given by Christ to the Apostles was restricted in its application by the limits of the Roman world itself, these limits being providential and not arbitrary; but it goes without saying that a limitation of this kind is not peculiar to the Christian world: Moslem expansion, for example, is necessarily confined within analogous limits and for the same reasons. Accordingly, although the Arabian polytheists were given the alternative of Islam or death, this principle was abandoned as soon as the frontiers of Arabia were left behind; thus the Hindus, who moreover are not monotheists,* although governed by Moslem monarchs for several centuries, were never subjected after their conquest to the alternative imposed not long before upon the Arab pagans. Another example is to be found in the traditional delimitation of the Hindu world. It must be added that the claim of Hinduism to universality, in conformity with the metaphysical and contemplative nature of this religion, is marked by a serenity not to be found in the Western theological outlook. The conception of *Sanātana Dharma,* the "Eternal [or Primordial] Law," is static and not dynamic, in the sense that it is an acknowledgment of fact and not an aspiration as in the case of the corresponding Semitic conceptions: the latter have their root in the idea that it is necessary to bring to mankind the true faith it does not yet possess, while,

---

* Monotheists are "The People of the Book" (*ahl al-Kitāb*), that is to say, Jews and Christians who have received Revelations in the spiritual line of Abraham. It seems almost superfluous to add that the Hindus, though not "monotheists" in the specifically Semitic sense, are certainly not "polytheists," since consciousness of metaphysical Unity throughout the indefinite multiplicity of forms is one of the most outstanding characteristics of the Hindu spirit.

according to the Hindu conception, the Brahmanic Tradition is the original Truth and Law that others no longer possess, either because what they have is only a fragment or because they have altered it, or even replaced it by errors; there is nevertheless no point in converting them, because, even though fallen from the *Sanātana Dharma,* they are not thereby excluded from salvation, being simply in spiritual conditions less favorable than those of the Hindus. From the Hindu standpoint, there is nothing in principle to prevent "barbarians" from being yogis or even *Avatāras;* in fact Hindus venerate without distinction Moslem, Buddhist, and Christian saints, and indeed were it otherwise the term *Mleccha Avatāra* ("Divine Descent among the Barbarians") would be meaningless; but it is considered that among non-Hindus saintliness will no doubt occur much more rarely than within the *Sanātana Dharma,* of which the ultimate sanctuary is the holy land of India.*

In this connection it might be asked whether the penetration by Islam onto the soil of India should not be regarded as an illegitimate encroachment from a religious point of view, and the same question arises regarding those parts of China and Southeast Asia that have become Moslem. To reply to this question it is necessary in the first place to dwell on matters that may appear somewhat remote, but that are nonetheless indispensable in this context. Before all else it is essential to take the following facts into account: if Hinduism has always adapted itself, as regards its spiritual life, to the cyclic conditions that it has had to face in the course of its historical existence, it has nevertheless always preserved its essentially primordial character. This is particularly so as regards its formal structure, notwithstanding the secondary modifications brought about by the force of events, such as, for example, the

---

* There has even been an "untouchable" in the south of India who was an *Avatāra* of Shiva, namely, the great spiritual master Tiruvalluvar, the "Divine," whose memory is still venerated in Tamil country, and who has left an inspired book, the *Kural.*

The equivalent of the Hindu conception of *Sanātana Dharma* is to be found in certain passages of the Koran that state that there is no people to whom God has not sent a Prophet; the exoteric induction according to which all other peoples have rejected or forgotten their own particular Revelation has no foundation in the Koran itself.

almost indefinite splitting up of the castes; but at a certain cyclic moment this primordiality, impregnated as it is with contemplative serenity, was overshadowed by the increasingly marked preponderance of the passional element in the general mentality, in accordance with the law of decline that governs every cycle of terrestrial humanity. Hinduism thus came to lose some of its actuality or vitality in the gradual process of moving away from its origins, and neither spiritual readaptations such as the advent of the tantric and "bhaktic" ways, nor social readaptations such as the splitting up of the castes already referred to, sufficed to eliminate the disproportion between the primordiality inherent in the religion and a mentality increasingly linked to the passions.* However, there could be no question of Hinduism being replaced by a religious form more

* One of the signs of this obscuration is the literal interpretation of symbolic texts on transmigration, which gives rise to the reincarnationist theory; this same literalism, when applied to sacred images, gives rise to idolatry. Were it not for this "pagan" aspect, which in practice taints the cult of many Hindus of lower caste, Islam could not have made so deep an impression in the Hindu world. If, in order to defend the reincarnationist interpretations of the Hindu Scriptures, reliance is placed on the literal sense of the texts, it would be only logical to interpret everything therein in a literal way, and one would then arrive not only at a crude anthropomorphism, but also at a crude and monstrous adoration of sensory nature, whether in the shape of elements, animals, or objects; the fact that many Hindus do interpret the symbolism of transmigration according to the letter proves nothing else than an intellectual decadence, almost normal in the *Kali-yuga,* and foreseen by the Scriptures. Moreover, in Western religions also, texts on posthumous conditions should not be understood literally: for example, the "fire" of hell is not a physical fire, the "bosom of Abraham" is not his corporeal bosom, the "feast" of which Christ speaks is not made up of terrestrial foods; moreover, if reincarnation were a reality, all the monotheistic doctrines would be false, since they never situate posthumous states on this earth; but all these considerations are relatively insignificant in view of the metaphysical impossibility of reincarnation. Even admitting that a great Hindu saint might adopt a literalist interpretation of the Scriptures in relation to a cosmological question such as transmigration, that still would prove nothing against his spirituality, since it is possible to conceive of a knowledge that is quite detached from purely cosmological realities, and that consists of an exclusively synthetic and inward vision of the Divine Reality. The same would not apply in the case of a person whose vocation was to expound or comment on a specifically cosmological doctrine, but, by reason of the spiritual laws that govern our times, such a vocation could hardly arise now within the framework of a particular religion.

adapted to the particular conditions of the second half of the *Kali-yuga,* since the Hindu world as a whole has obviously no need of a total transformation, the Revelation of *Manu Vaivasvata* having retained to a sufficient degree the actuality or vitality that justifies the persistence of a civilization. Nevertheless, it must be recognized that a paradoxical situation has arisen in Hinduism that may be described by saying that as a whole it is living or actual, while being no longer so in certain of its secondary aspects. Each of these two realities was bound to have its own consequences in the exterior world: the consequence of the vitality of Hinduism was the invincible resistance that it put up to Buddhism and Islam, while the consequence of its enfeeblement was, firstly, the Buddhist wave that came only to depart, and secondly, the expansion, and particularly the stabilization, of the Islamic civilization on the soil of India.

But the presence of Islam in India can be explained not only by the fact that being the youngest of the great Revelations,* it is better adapted than Hinduism to the general conditions of the last millennium of the Dark Age—or in other words, by the fact that it takes better into account the preponderance of the element of passion in the souls of men—but also by the following circumstance: the cyclic decline brings with it a quasi-general obscuration, which goes hand in hand with a more or less considerable growth of population, particularly at the lower levels; but this decadence implies a complementary and compensatory cosmic tendency that will act within the social collectivity for the purpose of restoring, at least symbolically, the original quality. In the first place, the collectivity will be pierced, as it were, by exceptions, and this process will run parallel with its quantitative growth, as if the qualitative (or "sattvic," conforming to pure Being) element within the collectivity were concentrated on particular cases by a compensatory effect of the quantitative expansion; and secondly, because of the same

---

* Islam is the last Revelation of the present cycle of terrestrial humanity, just as Hinduism represents the Primordial Tradition, though without identifying itself with it purely and simply, being in fact merely its most direct branch; consequently between these two religious forms there is a cyclic or cosmic relationship that, as such, is in no way fortuitous.

cosmic law of compensation, the spiritual means will become more and more easy for those who are qualified and whose aspirations are serious. This law comes into play because the human cycle for which the castes are valid is nearing its end, and for this reason the compensation in question tends not merely to restore, symbolically and within certain limits, the castes as they were in the beginning, but even humanity as it was before the institution of the castes. These considerations will make it possible to understand the positive and providential function of Islam in India; first of all, it is there to absorb elements that, owing to the new cyclic conditions referred to above, are no longer in their proper place in the Hindu religion—we are thinking more particularly of elements belonging to the higher castes, the *Dwijas*—and secondly, to absorb those elements of the elite that are to be found among the lower castes, who are thus rehabilitated in a kind of primordial indifferentiation. Islam, with the synthetic simplicity of its form and spiritual means, is an instrument providentially adapted to close up certain fissures appearing in more ancient and archaic civilizations, and to attract and neutralize by its presence the germs of subversion contained in these fissures, and it is in this way—but in this way only—that the domains of these civilizations have partially entered into the providential sphere of Islamic expansion.

Finally, at the risk of being somewhat repetitive, we will examine this question from a rather different angle, so as not to neglect any possible aspect. The Brahmanic possibility must in the end be manifested in all the castes, including even the *Shūdras,* not merely in a purely analogous way, as has always been the case, but on the contrary, directly; the reason for this is that the lowest caste, though but a part in the beginning, has become a whole toward the end of the cycle, and this whole is comparable to a social totality; the higher elements of this totality have become, so to speak, normal exceptions. In other words, the present state of the castes would appear to reflect, to a certain extent and symbolically, the primordial indistinction, the intellectual differences between the castes having become more and more attenuated. The lower castes, who have become very numerous, now in fact constitute a whole people and consequently embrace every human possibility, while the higher castes, who have not multiplied in the same proportion, have suffered a decay that is the more marked because "the corruption of the best is the worst" (*corruptio optimi pessima*). It must, however, be emphasized, in order to avoid misunderstanding, that from the collective and hereditary standpoint the elite among the lower castes remain "exceptions that prove the rule," and for this reason cannot legitimately mingle with the higher castes, though this does not prevent their being individually qualified to follow the ways normally reserved for the noble castes. Thus the system of castes, which for thousands of years has been a factor of equilibrium, necessarily reveals certain fissures at the end of the *mahā-yuga,* like the disequilibrium of the terrestrial environment itself. As regards the positive aspect implied by these fissures, it arises from the same cosmic law of compensation that Ibn 'Arabī had in mind when he said—in accordance, moreover, with various sayings of the Prophet—that at the end of time the flames of hell would grow cold; and it is this same law that inspired the Prophet to say that toward the end of the world he who accomplishes but a tenth of what Islàm exacted in the beginning will be saved. All that has just been said naturally applies to humanity as a whole and not only to the Hindu castes; and as for the fissures the existence of which we have noted in the outer structure of Hinduism, quite analogous phenomena appear in one degree or another in every traditional form.

With regard to the functional analogy between Buddhism and Islam in relation to Hinduism—the two first-mentioned religions having the same negative and the same positive role in relation to the latter—Buddhists, whether Mahayanist or Hinayanist, are fully aware of it, for they see in the Moslem invasions of India a punishment for the persecutions that they themselves had to suffer at the hands of the Hindus.

3

After this digression, which was necessary in order to explain an important aspect of Moslem expansion, we will return to a more fundamental question, that of the duality of meanings inherent in the Divine injunctions concerning human things. This duality is prefigured in the very name of "Jesus Christ": "Jesus"—like "Gotama" and "Mohammed"—indicates the limited and relative aspect of the manifestation of the Spirit, and denotes the support of this manifestation; "Christ"—like "Buddha" and *Rasūl Allāh*"—indicates the Universal Reality of this same manifestation, that is to say, the Word as such; and this duality of aspects is likewise found in the distinction between the human and Divine natures of Christ, though the viewpoint of theology does not permit of all the consequences being drawn from this distinction.

Now if the Apostles conceived Christ and their mission in an absolute sense, it must not be assumed that the reason for this lies in some intellectual limitation on their part, and it is necessary to take into account the fact that in the Roman world Christ and His Church possessed a unique and therefore "relatively absolute" character. This expression, which looks like a contradiction in terms, and which logically is so, nevertheless corresponds to a reality: the Absolute must also be reflected "as such" in the relative, and this reflection then becomes, in relation to other relativities, "relatively absolute." For example, the difference between two errors can only be relative, at least from the standpoint of their falsity, one being merely more false—or less false—than the other; on the other hand, the difference between error and truth will be absolute, but in a relative way only, that is to say, without going beyond the realm of relativities, since error, being only a more or less pronounced negation of truth cannot be absolutely independent of the latter; in other words, error, not being anything positive in itself, cannot be opposed to truth as one equal to another and as an independent reality. This makes it possible to understand why there cannot be such a thing as the "absolutely relative": the latter would be pure nothingness, and as such could have no kind of existence. As we were saying, in the Roman world Christ and His Church possessed a unique and therefore "relatively absolute" character; in other words, the principial, metaphysical, and symbolic unicity of Christ, of the Redemption, and of the Church was necessarily expressed by a unicity of fact on the terrestrial plane. If the Apostles were not called upon to formulate the metaphysical limits that every fact carries with it by definition, and if in consequence they were not called upon to take account of religious universality on the ground of facts, this does not mean that their spiritual Science did not include knowledge of this universality in principle, even though this knowledge was not actualized as regards possible applications to determined contingencies. For example, an eye capable of seeing a circle is capable of seeing all forms, even though they may not be present and the eye is looking only at the circle. The question of knowing what the Apostles or Christ himself would have said had they met a being such as the Buddha is quite pointless, for things of this kind never happen, since they would be contrary to cosmic laws; perhaps it is not too much to say that no one has ever heard of meetings taking place between great saints belonging to different civilizations. In the world destined to receive their radiation, the Apostles were, by definition, a unique group. Even if the presence in their sphere of action of Essenian, Pythagorean, or other initiates must be admitted, the inconspicuous light of these very small minorities must necessarily have been drowned in the radiance of the light of Christ, and the Apostles were not concerned with these few men who were "whole," for "I am not come to call the righteous, but sinners . . ." (Matt. 9:13). From a rather different point of view, though one connected with the same principle of religious delimitation, it may be noted that according to a rather enigmatic passage from the Acts of the Apostles (16:6–8), Saint Paul, who for Christianity was the primordial architect of expansion, as Omar was at a later date for Islam, avoided penetrating into the providential domain of this last form of Revelation. Without insisting on the fact that the limits of these fields of expansion obviously do not have the precise definition of political frontiers, we will merely add that the return of the Apostle of the Gentiles toward the West has nonetheless a symbolical value, not so much in relation to Islam as in relation to the delimitation of the Christian world itself; moreover, the manner in which this episode is related, with references to the intervention of the Holy Ghost and the "Spirit of Jesus," but with no mention of the causes of these inspirations, makes it impossible to accept the view that the reasons for the Apostle's having refrained from preaching and for his abrupt return were purely external ones with no principial significance, or that the episode in question was an ordinary incident of his journeyings.* Lastly, the fact that the province where this intervention of the Spirit occurred was called "Asia" adds further to the symbolical significance of the circumstances in question.

* We wish to state clearly that if we make use of specific examples instead of keeping to principles and generalities, this is never with the intention of convincing opponents whose minds are already made up, but simply to enable those who wish to understand to get a glimpse of certain aspects of reality; it is for the latter alone that we are writing, and we decline to enter into polemics that would have no interest for our eventual contradictors or for ourself. It must be added that we have not touched on the facts quoted by way of example for the sake of historical interest, for these facts do not matter in themselves, but solely insofar as they assist in the understanding of transcendent truths, which for their part are never dependent on facts.

6

The Ternary Aspect of Monotheism

1

The transcendent unity of the religious forms is illustrated in a particularly instructive manner by the reciprocal relationships existing between the three great so-called "monotheistic" religions, and this is precisely because these three religions alone present themselves in the form of irreconcilable exoterisms. First of all, however, it is necessary to make a clear distinction between what may be called symbolical truth and objective truth. To illustrate this distinction we may take as an example the arguments of Christianity and Buddhism with regard to the religious forms from which they may be said to have respectively issued, namely, Judaism in the first case and Hinduism in the second. These arguments are "symbolically true," in the sense that the rejected forms are considered not in themselves and from the standpoint of their intrinsic truth but solely in certain contingent and negative aspects that are due to a partial decadence; the rejection of the *Veda* therefore corresponds to a truth insofar as this Scripture is viewed exclusively as the symbol of a sterile erudition that was widespread in the time of Buddha, and the rejection by St. Paul of the Jewish Law was justified insofar as the latter corresponded to a Pharisaic formalism lacking spiritual life. If a new Revelation may thus justifiably depreciate religious values of an earlier origin, it is because it is independent of these values and has no need of them, since it possesses equivalent values of its own and is therefore entirely self-sufficient.

This truth likewise applies within one and the same religious form, for instance, with respect to the antinomy between the Latin and Greek Churches; the schism is a contingency that can in no way affect the intrinsic and essential reality of the two Churches. The schism in question is not, moreover, any more than the Moslem schism that gave birth to Shiite Islam, due solely to the will of individuals, whatever the appearances may be, but springs from the very nature of the religion that it divides outwardly, though not inwardly. Owing to ethnic and other contingencies, the spirit of the religion may require different, though always orthodox, adaptations. The same considerations do not, of course, apply in the case of heresies, which divide the religion both inwardly and outwardly—though unable to effect a real division, since error is not a part of truth—and which instead of merely being incompatible on the formal plane with other aspects of a self-same truth, are false in themselves.

Let us now consider as a whole the question of the spiritual and cyclic homogeneity of the religions. Monotheism, which embraces the Jewish, Christian, and Islamic religions, is essentially based on a dogmatic conception of the Divine Unity (or "Nonduality"). If we speak of this conception as being dogmatic, this is to indicate that it is accompanied by an exclusion of every other point of view, failing which an exoteric application, which is the justification for all dogmas, would not be possible. We have previously seen that this restriction, though necessary for the vitality of the exoteric forms, is fundamentally responsible for the limitation inherent in the theological point of view as such; in other words, the theological viewpoint is characterized by an incompatibility within its own field between conceptions that in form are apparently opposed to one another, whereas in the case of purely metaphysical or initiatory doctrines, formulations that appear contradictory are not in fact mutually exclusive, nor do they interfere with one another in any way.*

---

* The fact that certain data from the Scriptures are interpreted unilaterally by the representatives of exoterism proves that their limitative speculations are not entirely disinterested, as has already been shown in the chapter on exoterism. In fact, the esoteric interpretation of a Revelation is admitted by

The monotheistic religion belonged originally to the entire nomadic branch of the Semitic group, a branch that, having issued from Abraham, was subdivided into two secondary branches, one issuing from Isaac and the other from Ishmael, and it was not until the time of Moses that monotheism took a Judaic form; it was Moses who, at a time when the religion of Abraham was growing dim among the Ishmaelites, was called upon to give monotheism a powerful support by linking it in a certain manner with the people of Israel, who thus became its guardians; but this adaptation, however necessary and providential it may have been, was also bound to lead to a restriction of the outward form, owing to the "particularist" tendency inherent in each people. It may thus be said that Judaism annexed monotheism and made it the possession of Israel, with the result that under this form the heritage of Abraham was henceforth inseparable from all the secondary adaptations and all the ritual and social consequences implicit in the Mosaic Law.

As a result of being thus canalized and crystallized in Judaism, monotheism acquired a historical character, though the word "his-

---

exoterism whenever it serves to confirm the latter, and it is, on the contrary, arbitrarily passed over whenever it might prove harmful to that outward dogmatism that is the refuge of sentimental individualism. Thus the truth represented by Christ, which by its form belongs to Jewish esoterism, is invoked in condemnation of an excessive formalism in Judaism; but those who invoke it carefully refrain from applying this same truth to every form without exception, including the Christian. Again, according to St. Paul's Epistle to the Romans (3:27–4:17), man is justified by faith and not by works; however, according to the General Epistle of St. James (2:14–26), man is justified by works and not by faith alone; both cite Abraham as an example. If these two texts had belonged to different religions, or even to two reciprocally schismatic branches of a single religion, the theologians on either side would no doubt have set about proving their incompatibility; but since they belong to one and the same religion, efforts are made, on the contrary, to prove their perfect compatibility. Why is it that people are reluctant to admit Revelations other than their own? "God cannot contradict Himself," it will be said, though this is merely begging the question. There are two alternatives: either it must be admitted that God really contradicts Himself, in which case no Revelation will be accepted; or else it must be admitted, since there is no other choice, that the contradictions are but an appearance, but then there will be no further justification for rejecting a foreign Revelation simply because at first sight it appears to be in contradiction with the Revelation of which the validity is admitted a priori.

torical" should not here be understood exclusively in its ordinary outward meaning, which would be incompatible with the sacred nature of Israel. It is this absorption of the original religion by the Jewish people that makes it permissible to distinguish outwardly the monotheism of Moses from that of the Patriarchs, though such a distinction does not, of course, concern the domain of doctrine. The historical character of Judaism, owing to its very nature, had a consequence that was not inherent in the original monotheism—not, at least, in the same form. This was the Messianic idea, and this idea is accordingly linked to the Mosaic Tradition.

These few observations concerning the original monotheism, its adaptation by Moses, its annexation by Judaism, and its concretization in the Messianic idea, are sufficient to enable us to proceed to a consideration of the organic role played by Christianity in the monotheistic cycle. We may say, therefore, that Christianity in its turn absorbed all the doctrinal heritage of monotheism into the affirmation of the Messiah, and that it was entirely within its rights in doing so—if one may thus express it—since it was the legitimate fruition of the Judaic form. The Messiah, having to realize in His own person the Divine Will from which monotheism issued, necessarily transcended a form that was incapable of allowing the latter to realize its mission fully. In order that He might effect this dissolution of a transitory form, it was necessary, as we have just indicated, that, as Messiah, He should possess to an eminent degree the authority inherent in the Tradition whose ultimate word He was, and it is for this reason that He had to be "greater" than Moses and "before" Abraham. These affirmations clearly indicate a direct identity between the Messiah and God, and show that a Christianity that denies the Divinity of Christ denies the reason for its own existence.

We have said that the "avataric" person of the Messiah entirely absorbed the monotheistic doctrine, which means that Christ had to be not only the termination of historical Judaism, at least in a certain respect and in a certain measure, but also for that very reason the support of monotheism and the temple of the Divine Presence. This extreme historical positivity of Christ brought with it, however, in its turn a limitation of the religious form, just as had happened in the case of Judaism, where Israel played the predominant role that was later to devolve upon the Messiah, a role that was necessarily restrictive and limitative from the point of view of the realization of integral monotheism. It is here that Islam enters in, and it remains for us to consider its position and significance in the monotheistic cycle.*

However, before going into this subject, there remains to be considered another aspect of the question with which we have been dealing. The Gospels relate the following saying of Christ: "The law and the prophets were until John: since that time the Kingdom of God is preached, and every man presseth into it"; and the Gospels also relate that at the moment of Christ's death the veil of the Temple was rent in twain from the top to the bottom; this and the saying just quoted both indicate that the coming of Christ put a final term to the religion of Moses. But it may well be objected that the Mosaic religion, insofar as it is the Word of God, cannot by any means be annulled, since "our Torah is for all eternity, nothing can be added to it and nothing taken away from it" (Maimonides); how, therefore, is one to reconcile the abrogation of the religion of Moses, or rather of the "glorious" cycle of its terrestrial existence, with the "eternity" of the Mosaic Revelation? First, it must be understood that this abrogation, although quite real in the realm to which it relates, is nonetheless relative, whereas the intrinsic reality of the Mosaic religion is absolute, because Divine. It is this Divine quality that is necessarily opposed to the suppression of a Revelation, at least for so long as the doctrinal and ritual form of the latter remains intact, a condition

---

* The perspective we have just outlined brings to mind Joachim of Floris who attributed to each Person of the Trinity a predominant position in relation to a certain part of the religious cycle of the Christian perspective: the Father dominated the Old Law, the Son the New Law, and the Holy Ghost the last phase of the Christian cycle that began with the new monastic orders founded by St. Francis and St. Dominic. The asymmetry of these correspondences will at once be apparent: the author of this theory must have been ignorant (whether such ignorance was real or professed) of the existence of Islam, which according to Islamic dogma actually corresponds to this reign of the Paraclete; but it is nevertheless true that the period that according to Joachim of Floris was placed under the special influence of the Holy Ghost did see a renewal of spirituality in the West.

that was fulfilled in the case of the religion of Moses, as is shown by the fact that Christ conformed to it.* The abrogation of the Mosaic religion by Christ springs from a Divine Volition, but the intangible permanence of that same religion is of a still profounder order, since it derives from the Divine Essence itself, of which this Volition is simply a particular manifestation, just as a wave is a particular manifestation of water, the nature of which it cannot modify. The Divine Volition manifested by Christ could affect only a particular mode of the religion of Moses and not its "eternal" quality; consequently, although the Real Presence—the *Shekhīnah*—had left the Holy of Holies in the Temple of Jerusalem, this Divine Presence has always continued to dwell in Israel, no longer, it is true, like an unquenchable fire localized in a sanctuary, but like a flint that, though not permanently manifesting fire,

---

* It is, however, important to observe that the decadence of Jewish esoterism at the time of Christ—for example, Nicodemus, a "master in Israel," was unacquainted with the mystery of spiritual rebirth!—made it permissible from the standpoint of the new Revelation to regard the Mosaic religion in its entirety as an exclusive and therefore, as it were, "massive" exoterism, a way of looking at things that has nevertheless only an accidental and provisional value, since it is limited in its application to the origins of Christianity. However that may be, the Mosaic Law was not to govern access to the new Mysteries, as would have been the function of an exoterism in relation to an esoterism of which it was the complement, and another exoterism was established for the new religion, though at the cost of difficulties of adaptation and of interferences that continued for centuries.

Meanwhile, Judaism for its part reconstituted and readapted its own exoterism in the new cycle of its history, the Diaspora, and this process appears to have been to some extent correlative to the development of Christianity, thanks to the copious influx of spirituality accompanying the manifestation of the Word in the person of Christ. The influence of this manifestation made itself felt directly or indirectly, openly or in secret, throughout the whole neighboring environment. This accounts, on the one hand, for the disappearance during the first century of the Christian cycle of the ancient Mysteries, a part of which was absorbed by Christian esoterism itself, and on the other hand, for the irradiation of spiritual forces in the Mediterranean traditions during the same period, for example, in Neo-Platonism. As regards Judaism, there existed until modern times, and perhaps still exists in certain places, a genuine esoteric tradition, whatever may have been the exact date of the revival that took place subsequently to the manifestation of Christ and the beginning of the new religious cycle, the Diaspora, and whatever may have been the part later played by Islam in its turn in relation to both Judaism and Christianity.

nevertheless contains it virtually, with the possibility of manifesting it from time to time.

2

Monotheism contained, in Judaism and Christianity, two great antagonistic expressions which Islam, although itself necessarily antagonistic in relation to these two forms, recapitulated in a certain manner by harmonizing the Judaeo-Christian antagonism in a synthesis that marked the term of the development and integral realization of monotheism. That this was so is confirmed by the simple fact that Islam is the third aspect of this religious current; that is to say, it represents the number *3,* which is the number of harmony, whereas the number *2* represents an alternative and is not therefore self-sufficient, being compelled either to reduce itself to unity through the absorption of one of its terms by the other or to recreate this unity by the production of a new unity. These two methods of realizing unity are in fact achieved by Islam, which itself provides the solution of the Judaeo-Christian antagonism from which in a certain sense it may be said to have issued, and which it annuls by reducing it to the pure monotheism of Abraham. In this connection, Islam might be compared to a Judaism that had not rejected Christianity, or to a Christianity that had not denied Judaism; but if its attitude can be characterized in this way insofar as it was the product of Judaism and Christianity, it stands outside this duality insofar as it identifies itself with the origin of the latter, through its rejection of the Judaic "development," on the one hand, and the Christian "transgression," on the other; and through its having restored to the place of central importance, acquired first by the Jewish people and then by Christ, the fundamental affirmation of monotheism, namely, the Unity of God. As a condition of being able thus to transcend Messianism, it was necessary for Islam to place itself at a point of view that was different from that of the latter, and to reduce the latter to its own point of view in order to integrate it within itself; hence the integration of Christ in the line of Prophets, which extends from Adam to Mohammed. It goes without saying that Islam, like the two preceding religions, came into being through a direct intervention of the Divine Will from which monotheism issued, and that the Prophet had to reflect, according to a special possibility and with a corresponding mode of realization, the essential Messianic truth inherent in the original or Abrahamic monotheism. In a certain sense, Islam can be called the Abrahamic reaction against the annexation of monotheism by Israel on the one hand and by the Messiah on the other. Although metaphysically the two points of view are by no means mutually exclusive, on the exoteric plane they cannot be realized simultaneously and can only be affirmed by means of antagonistic dogmas that divide the outward aspect of integral monotheism.

If in a certain respect Judaism and Christianity present a single front against Islam, Christianity and Islam in their turn are opposed to Judaism, in consequence of their tendency toward a full realization of the monotheistic doctrine. We have seen, however, that in the case of the Christian form this tendency was limited by the predominance given to the Messianic idea, which is only of secondary importance from the standpoint of pure monotheism. The legislative framework of Judaism was broken by an exteriorization, here necessary and legitimate, of certain esoteric conceptions, and was absorbed in a manner of speaking by the "next world," in conformity with the formula *Regnum meum non est de hoc mundo.* The social order was replaced by the spiritual, the sacraments of the Church being the form of legislation appropriate to the latter order. But since this spiritual legislation does not meet social requirements, it was necessary to have recourse to heterogeneous legislative elements, which created a cultural dualism that was very harmful to the Christian world. Islam re-established a sacred legislation for "this world," and in this way rejoined Judaism, while at the same time reaffirming the universality that Christianity had affirmed beforehand when breaking the husk of the Mosaic Law.

One thing more remains to be said: the equilibrium between the two Divine aspects of Justice and Mercy constitutes the very essence of the Mohammedan Revelation, in which it rejoins the Abrahamic Revelation. As for the Christian Revelation, if it affirms its superiority over the Mosaic Revelation it is because the Divine

Mercy is principially and ontologically "anterior" to the Divine Justice, as is attested by this inscription on the Throne of Allāh: "Verily, My Mercy precedeth My Wrath" (*Inna Raḥmatī sabaqat Ghaḍabī*). The monotheism revealed to Abraham possessed esoterism and exoterism in perfect equilibrium, and in a certain measure in their primordial indistinction, though there can only be a question here of a primordiality that is relative to the religions belonging to the Semitic stock. With Moses exoterism, so to speak, became the religion, in the sense that it determined the form of the latter without, however, affecting its essence; with Christ the reverse happened, and it was esoterism that in a certain manner became the religion in its turn; finally, with Mohammed the initial equilibrium is re-established and the cycle of the monotheistic religion is closed. These alternations in the integral Revelation of monotheism proceeded from the very nature of the latter and are not therefore imputable to contingent circumstances alone. Since both the "letter" and the "spirit" were synthetically comprised in the primordial or Abrahamic monotheism, they were bound to become crystallized in some fashion, by differentiation and successively, during the course of the cycle of the monotheistic Revelation; thus the religion of Abraham manifested the undifferentiated equilibrium of "letter" and "spirit," the religion of Moses the "letter," Chrisitianity the "spirit," and Islam the differentiated equilibrium of these two aspects of the Revelation.

Every religion is necessarily an adaptation, and adaptation implies limitation. If that is true of the purely metaphysical religions, it is still more true of the exoteric religions, which represent adaptations for the sake of more limited mentalities.* These limita-

* If one is justified in saying that the mentality of Western peoples, including in this respect the peoples of the Near East, is in some ways more limited than the mentality of most Eastern peoples, this is primarily because of the intrusion of passion in the sphere of the intelligence; hence the tendency of Westerners to regard created things only under one aspect, that of "plain fact," and their lack of aptitude for the intuitive contemplation of the cosmic and universal essences that permeate forms; this intrusion also explains the need for an abstract theism as a protection against the danger of idolatry as well as against that of pantheism. The mentality in question, owing to cyclic causes, has for centuries been becoming more and more widespread among all peoples, and this explains, on the one hand, the relative ease with which

tions must needs be found in one manner or another in the origins of the religious forms, and it is inevitable that they should be manifested in the course of the development of these forms, becoming most marked at the end of their cycle, to which they themselves necessarily contribute. If these limitations are necessary for the vitality of a religion, they remain nonetheless limitations with the consequences that that implies. The heterodox doctrines themselves are indirect consequences of this need for curtailing the amplitude of the religious form and for limiting it in proportion with the advance of the Dark Age. It could not indeed be otherwise, even in the case of the sacred symbols, because only the infinite, eternal, and formless Essence is absolutely pure and inviolable, and because Its transcendence must be made manifest by the dissolution of forms as well as by Its radiation through them.

---

religious conversions are made among peoples whose civilization is purely mythological or metaphysical, and on the other hand, the providential nature of Moslem expansion within the domains of these civilizations.

7

Christianity and Islam

1

We have seen that among the branches issuing more or less directly from the Primordial Tradition, Christianity and Islam represent the spiritual heritage of this Tradition according to different points of view. This immediately raises the question as to what exactly is represented by a "point of view" as such. No difficulty can arise in this connection on the plane of physical vision, where the point of view determines a perspective that is always perfectly coordinated and necessary, and where things change their aspect whenever the observer alters his standpoint, although the elements of vision, namely, the eye, light, colors, forms, proportions, and situations in space, remain always the same. The starting point of vision may change, but not the vision in itself. Now if everybody admits that such is the case in the physical world, which is but a reflection of spiritual realities, how can it be denied that the same relations exist, or rather pre-exist, in the spiritual realm? Here, the heart, organ of Revelation, corresponds to the eye; the Divine Principle, dispenser of light, to the sun; the Intellect to light; and the Realities or Divine Essences to the objects of vision. But whereas, generally speaking, nothing will prevent a living being from changing his physical point of view, it is quite another matter with the spiritual point of view, which always transcends the individual and regarding which the will of the latter can only remain determinate and passive.

In order to understand a spiritual point of view, or what amounts to the same, a religious point of view, it is not sufficient, even with the best intentions, to attempt to establish correspondences between religious elements outwardly resembling one another. Such a procedure would be in danger of leading to a superficial synthesis of little value, though comparisons of this sort may nevertheless have their uses, on condition that they are not adopted as a point of departure and provided also that account is first taken of the inner constitution of the religions in question. In order to grasp a religious point of view, it is necessary to perceive the unity by which all its constituent elements are necessarily coordinated; this unity is the unity of the spiritual point of view that is the germ of the particular Revelation. Needless to say, the first cause of a Revelation cannot be assimilated to a point of view any more than light can be said to depend on the spatial situation of the eye; what constitutes every Revelation is the encounter of a unique Light with a limited and contingent sphere, which represents as it were a plane of spiritual reflection, in the absence of which there could be no question of Revelation.

Before entering into particulars concerning the relationship between Christianity and Islam, it should be observed that the Western mentality, in its positive qualities, is almost entirely of Christian essence. It does not lie within the power of men to rid themselves of so deep-seated a heredity by their own means, that is to say, by mere ideological expedients; their minds move in age-old grooves even when they invent errors. One cannot set aside this intellectual and mental formation, however weakened it may be. This being the case, and given that some remnant of the religious point of view survives unconsciously even among those who consider themselves freed from any attachment, or who, in their desire to be impartial, attempt to place themselves outside the Christian standpoint, how is it to be expected that the elements of other religions will be interpreted in their true sense? Is it not striking, for instance, that the opinions about Islam prevailing among the majority of Westerners are more or less identical, whether those who utter them profess to be Christians or pride themselves on no longer being so? Even the errors of philosophy would not be conceivable if they did not represent the negation of certain truths, and if those errors were not direct or indirect reactions against certain formal limitations of religion; from which it can be seen that no error, whatever may be its nature, can lay claim to complete independence with regard to the traditional conception that it rejects or disfigures.

A religion is an integral whole comparable to a living organism that develops according to necessary and exact laws; one might therefore call it a spiritual organism, or a social one in its most outward aspect. In any case, it is an organism and not a construction of arbitrary conventions; one cannot therefore legitimately consider the constituent elements of a religion independently of their inward unity, as if one were concerned with a mere collection of facts. This error is one, however, that is frequently committed even by those who judge without preconceived opinions but who nonetheless endeavor to establish correspondences from the outside, without perceiving that a religious element is always determined by the germ and starting point of the integral religion, and that a given element, a personality or a book, for example, can have a different significance from one religion to another.

To illustrate these remarks we are going to compare certain fundamental elements of the Christian and Islamic religions. The habitual want of comprehension of the ordinary representatives of either religion with regard to the other extends to almost insignificant details, such as, for instance, the term "Mohammedan" applied to Moslems, an expression that is an improper transposition of the term "Christian." The latter expression is perfectly applicable to the adherents of a religion that is based on Christ and that perpetuates Him in the Eucharist and the Mystical Body. The same does not, however, apply to Islam, which is not based directly on the Prophet but on the Koran, thus on an affirmation of Divine Unity, and which does not consist in a perpetuation of Mohammed but in a ritual and legislative conformity of man and society to the Koranic Law and therefore to Unity. On the other hand, the Arabic term *mushrikūn,* "associators" (of pseudo divinities with God), which alludes to the Christians, overlooks the fact that Christianity is not directly based on the idea of Unity and need not insist upon it, since its essential basis is the Mystery of Christ;

nevertheless, insofar as the term *mushrikūn* is sacred—in its Koranic significance—it is obviously the support of a truth that transcends the historical fact of the Christian religion. Moreover, facts do not play so important a part in Islam as they do in Christianity, of which the religious basis is essentially a fact and not an idea as in the case of Islam. This serves to show where lies the fundamental divergence between the two religious forms: for a Christian all depends on the Incarnation and the Redemption; Christ absorbs everything, even the idea of the Divine Principle, which appears under a Trinitarian aspect, as well as humanity, which becomes His Mystical Body or the Church militant, suffering and triumphant. For a Moslem all is centered in Allāh, the Divine Principle considered under the aspect of Unity* and of Transcendence, and in the state of conformity, of abandonment to Him: *Al-Islām*. The idea of God made Man is at the center of Christian doctrine; the Son, Second Person of the Trinity, is man universalized; Jesus Christ is God individualized. Islam does not give the same predominance to the mediator; the latter does not absorb everything, and it is exclusively the monotheistic conception of Divinity that takes the central place in Islamic doctrine and dominates it throughout.

The importance attached by Islam to the idea of Unity may appear superfluous and sterile from the Christian point of view and a sort of pleonasm with respect to the Judaeo-Christian tradition. One must, however, bear in mind that the spontaneity and vitality of the Islamic religion can by no means be the fruit of external borrowing and that the intellectual originality of the Moslems can only proceed from a Revelation. Whereas in Islam the idea of Unity is the support of all spirituality, and to a certain degree of all social applications, it is not the same in the case of Christianity; the central point of the latter, as we have already indicated, is the doctrine of the Incarnation and the Redemption, conceived in universal mode in the Trinity and having no human application other than in the sacraments and the participation in the Mystical

---

* It is expressly said in that Islamic credo, the *Fiqh al-Akbar* of Abū Ḥanīfah, that Allāh is unique, not in the sense of number, but in the sense that He is without associate.

Body of Christ. At no time, so far as may be judged from historical data, has Christianity had a social application in the full sense of the word; never has it entirely integrated human society; in the form of the Church it imposed itself on men without attaching them to itself by assigning to them functions that would permit them to participate more directly in its inner life; it has not sufficiently hallowed human acts; it has left the entire laity outside itself, assigning to it only a more or less passive participation in the religion. Such is the organization of the Christian world as seen from a Moslem point of view. In Islam every man is his own priest by the mere fact of being a Moslem; he is the patriarch, *imām,* or caliph of his family; in the latter is reflected the entire Islamic society. Man is in himself a unity; he is the image of the Creator whose vicar (*khalīfah*) he is on earth; he cannot accordingly be a layman. The family is also a unity; it is a society within a society, an impenetrable block*—like the Moslem himself, at once responsible and submissive, and like the whole Islamic world, which is of an almost incorruptible homogeneity and stability. Man, family, and society are cast according to the idea of Unity of which they are so many adaptations; they are unities as are Allāh and His Word, the Koran. Christians cannot lay claim to the idea of Unity in the same degree as Moslems; the idea of Redemption is not necessarily bound to the conception of Divine Unity and might be associated with a so-called "polytheistic" doctrine. As for Divine Unity, although it is theoretically admitted by Christians, it never appears as a dynamic element, and Christian holiness, the perfect participation in the Mystical Body of Christ, proceeds but indirectly from this idea. Christian doctrine, like Islamic, starts from a theistic idea, but expressly insists on the Trinitarian aspect of the Divinity. God becomes incarnate and redeems the world; the Principle descends into manifestation to re-establish a disturbed equilibrium.

* The supreme symbol of Islam, the Kaaba, is a square block; it expresses the number *4,* which is the number of stability. The Moslem can create his family with four wives; they represent the substance of the family or the social substance itself, and are withdrawn from public life, where man is by himself a complete unity. The Arab house is planned in accordance with the same idea: it is square, uniform, closed to the outside, ornamented within, and opens onto the court.

According to Islamic doctrine God affirms Himself by His Unity; He does not become incarnate by virtue of an inner distinction, nor does He redeem the world, He absorbs it through *Islām*. He does not descend into manifestation, He projects Himself therein, as the sun projects itself through its light; and it is this projection that permits humanity to participate in Him.

It happens not infrequently that Moslems, for whom the Koran is what Christ is for Christians, reproach the latter for not having a book equivalent to the Koran, that is to say, a book to which no other can be compared, at once doctrinal and legislative, and which is written in the actual language of the Revelation. They see in the multiplicity of the Gospels and other New Testament texts the mark of a division that is aggravated by the fact that these Scriptures have not been preserved in the language spoken by Jesus, but in a non-Semitic language, and have even been translated from the latter into another language equally foreign to the peoples issued from Abraham; indeed these texts can be translated into any foreign language. This confusion is analogous to that which leads Christians to reproach the Prophet for having been a mere mortal. Thus, if in Islam the Koran is the Divine Word, the latter is represented in Christianity not by the New Testament, but by the living presence of Christ in the Eucharist. The New Testament only plays the part of a support, just as the Prophet is only a support of the Divine Message and not the Message itself. The remembrance, the example, and the intercession of the Prophet are subordinate to the revealed Book.

Islam is a spiritual, religious, and social block;* the Church is not a block but a center. A lay Christian is by definition a peripheral being; a Moslem, by reason of his priestly function, is everywhere a central being within his own religion, and it matters little to him whether or not he is externally severed from the Moslem community; he always remains his own priest and an autonomous unity, at least in relation to matters within the sphere of

---

* A block, image of Unity. Unity is simple and consequently indivisible. According to an observation of a former highly placed English official in Egypt: "Islam cannot be reformed; a reformed Islam would no longer be Islam, it would be something else."

religion. From this is derived the fundamental conviction of a Moslem. The faith of a Christian is of another nature: it attracts and absorbs the soul rather than enfolding and penetrating it. Regarded from the Moslem point of view, which concerns us here, the Christian is only linked to his religion through the sacraments; he is always in the position of being relatively excluded and he maintains at all times a receptive attitude. In the supreme symbol of Christianity, the Cross, its arms branch off indefinitely from the center while remaining connected with it; the Kaaba, on the other hand, is reflected as a whole in the least of its parts, each one of which, by its substance and internal cohesion, is identical with the other parts and with the Kaaba itself.

The correspondences between religious elements that have been noted above do not exclude others that may exist from a different point of view. Thus the analogy between the New Testament and the Koran remains real in its own order, just as there is a necessary correspondence from a certain point of view between Christ and the Prophet; to deny this would be to maintain that there are resemblances without sufficient cause, therefore meaningless. But the superficial and even syncretic manner in which such correspondences are most often viewed, usually to the disadvantage of one or the other element under comparison, deprive the result of any true value. In reality, there are two kinds of religious correspondences: on the one hand, those based on what may be called the phenomenal nature of the elements of the religions in question, and on the other hand, those derived from the internal structure of those religions. In the first case, the element will be considered as a person, a book, a rite, an institution, or whatever it may be, and in the second case, this element will be considered from the point of view of its particular organic significance for the religion. This takes us back to the analogy existing between the spiritual and the physical points of view: according to the latter a given object always remains one and the same object, but it is able to change its aspect and importance according to different perspectives; and this law may readily be transposed to the spiritual sphere.

2

It is important to make it clear that in this chapter we have been exclusively concerned with religions as such, that is to say, as organisms, and not with their purely spiritual possibilities, which are identical in principle. It is obvious that from this point of view any question of preference is excluded; if Islam as a religious organism is more homogeneous and more intimately coherent than the Christian form, this is a relatively contingent matter. Likewise the solar nature of Christ cannot confer upon Christianity a superiority over Islam; we will explain the reason for this further on and need only recall here that from a certain standpoint each religious form is necessarily superior to others belonging to the same order, though only in some particular aspect of its manifestation and not in its essence or spiritual possibilities. To those who would judge the Islamic form on the basis of superficial and necessarily arbitrary comparisons with the Christian form, we would reply that Islam, given that it represents a possible spiritual perspective, is all that it should be to manifest this possibility; and we would say likewise that the Prophet, far from having been merely an imperfect imitator of Christ, was all that he should have been in order to realize the spiritual possibility represented by Islam. If the Prophet is not Christ and if in particular he appears under a more human aspect, it is because the reason for the existence of Islam does not reside in the idea of Christ or of the *Avatāra,* but in an idea that necessarily excludes this perspective. The idea thus realized by Islam and the Prophet is that of the Divine Unity, the absolutely transcendent aspect of which implies—for the created or manifested world—a corresponding aspect of imperfection. This explains why it has been permissible for Moslems from the very beginning to employ a human means such as war to establish their religious world, whereas in the case of Christianity several centuries had to elapse after the apostolic times before it became possible to use the same means, which is, moreover, indispensable for the propagation of a religion. As for the wars engaged in by the Companions of the Prophet, they represented ordeals undergone in view of what might be called the elaboration—or the crystallization—of the formal aspects of a new world. Hatred did not enter in, and the holy men who fought in this manner, far from fighting against individuals and for human interests, did so in the spirit of the teaching of the *Bhagavad-Gītā;* Krishna enjoined upon Arjuna to fight, not out of hatred nor even to conquer, but in order to fulfill his destiny as an instrument of the Divine plan and without attaching himself to the fruits of his actions.

This struggle between "points of view" at the time of the constitution of a religious world also reflects the "rivalry" between possibilities of manifestation at the time of the emergence from chaos that takes place at the origin of a cosmic world, a rivalry that is of course of a purely principial order. It was in the nature of Islam and of its mission that it should from the beginning have placed itself on political ground so far as its outward affirmation was concerned, whereas such an attitude would not only have been entirely contrary to the nature or mission of primitive Christianity, but also completely unrealizable in an environment as solid and stable as that of the Roman Empire. However, once Christianity had become a state religion, it was not merely able but even bound to enter the political arena in exactly the same way as Islam. The outward vicissitudes suffered by Islam after the death of the Prophet are certainly not attributable to a spiritual insufficiency, being simply blemishes inherent in the political realm as such. The fact that Islam was established outwardly by human means had its sole cause in the Divine Will, which precisely excluded all esoteric interference in the earthly structure of the new religious form. On the other hand, so far as the difference between Christ and the Prophet is concerned, we would add that great spiritual men, whatever their respective degrees, manifest either a sublimation or a norm; to the first group belong Buddha and Christ as well as all those saints who were monks or hermits, while to the second belong Abraham, Moses, and Mohammed, together with all saints living in the world, such as the royal and warrior saints. The attitude of the former corresponds to the words of Christ, "My Kingdom is not of this world," the attitude of the latter to the words, "Thy Kingdom come."

Those who believe it their duty to deny the legitimacy of the Prophet of Islam on moral grounds forget that the only question to be answered is whether or not Mohammed was inspired by God, it being quite irrelevant whether or not he was comparable to Jesus or conformed to some established morality. When one remembers that it was God who allowed polygamy to the Hebrews and commanded Moses to have the population of Canaan put to the sword, it is clear that the question of the morality of such conduct is in no way involved; what alone counts in every case is the fact of the Divine Will, the object of which is invariable, but the means or modes of which vary by reason of the Infinity of its Possibility and, secondarily, because of the limitless diversity of contingencies. Christians readily blame the Prophet for actions such as the destruction of the tribe of the Qurayẓa, but they forget that any Prophet of Israel would have acted in a still sterner way than he, and they would do well to recall how Samuel, by the order of God, acted toward the Amalekites and their king. The case of the Qurayẓa is also like that of the Pharisees in that it provides an example of the "discernment of spirits" that takes place automatically, as it were, upon contact with a manifestation of Light. However neutral an individual may appear so long as he is placed in a chaotic or undifferentiated environment—such as, for example, the Near Eastern world at the time of Mohammed, or indeed any environment in which a religious readaptation is about to take place—and however attenuated or obscured the fundamental tendency of the individual may appear in an environment of spiritual indifference such as we have just described, this tendency will spontaneously be actualized when faced with the alternative presented upon contact with the Light; and this explains why it is that when the gates of Heaven are opened by the lightning flash of Revelation, the gates of Hell open too, just as in the sensory world a light projects a shadow.

If Mohammed had been a false prophet, there is no reason why Christ should not have spoken of him as he spoke of Antichrist; but if Mohammed is a true Prophet, the passages referring to the Paraclete must inevitably concern him—not exclusively but eminently—for it is inconceivable that Christ, when speaking of the future, should have passed over in silence a manifestation of such magnitude. The same reasoning excludes a priori the possibility that Christ, when making his predictions, intended to include Mohammed under the general denomination of "false prophets," for in the history of our era Mohammed is in no sense a typical example among others of the same kind, but on the contrary, a unique and incomparable apparition.* If he had been one of the false prophets announced by Christ, he would have been followed by others, and there would exist in our day a multitude of false religions subsequent to Christ and comparable in importance and extension to Islam. The spirituality to be found within Islam from its origins up to our days is an incontestable fact, and "by their fruits ye shall know them." Moreover, it will be recalled

---

* If greatness of design, economy of means, and immensity of achievement are the three measures of the genius of man, who will dare, on the human plane, to compare any of the great men of modern history with Mohammed? The most famous of them have done no more than stir up arms, laws, and empires; when they have founded anything, they have founded only material powers that often have crumbled before them. Mohammed stirred up armies, legislatures, empires, peoples, dynasties, millions of men over a third of the inhabited globe; but further, he stirred up ideas, beliefs, and souls. Upon a book, each letter of which has become law, he has founded a spiritual nationality that embraces peoples of every language and every race, and as the indelible characteristic of this Moslem nationality he has impressed upon it hatred of false gods and love of the one and immaterial God. [Lamartine, *Histoire de la Turquie*]

The Arab conquest, which flooded simultaneously both Europe and Asia, is without precedent; the rapidity of its successes can only be compared with the rapidity of the establishment of the Mongol empires of Attila, Genghis Khan, or Tamerlane. But these were as ephemeral as the Islamic conquest was durable. This religion still has followers today in almost all the countries where it was imposed under the first Caliphs. The lightning speed of its diffusion is truly miraculous when compared with the slow progress of Christianity. [H. Pirenne, *Mahomet et Charlemagne*]

Force had no part in the propagation of the Koran, for the Arabs always left those they conquered free to keep their religion. If Christian peoples became converted to the religion of their vanquishers, it was because the new conquerors showed themselves more just than their former masters, and because their religion was of a greater simplicity than the one taught to them up to that moment. . . . Far from being imposed by force, the Koran was spread only through persuasion. . . . Persuasion alone could induce peoples who conquered the Arabs at a later date, such as the Turks and the Mongols, to adopt it. In India, where the Arabs in reality but passed through, the Koran is so widely diffused that it can count today [1884] more than fifty million adherents. Their number increases daily. . . . The diffusion of the Koran in China has been no less wide. Although the Arabs have never conquered the smallest part of the Celestial Empire, there exists therein today a Moslem population of more then twenty millions. [G. le Bon, *La Civilisation des Arabes*]

that the Prophet in his doctrine has testified to the second coming of Christ without attributing to himself any glory, unless it be that of being the last Prophet of the cycle; and history proves that he spoke the truth, no comparable manifestation having followed after him.

Finally it is indispensable to say a few words concerning the Islamic attitude toward sexuality. If Moslem morality differs from the Christian—which is not the case in regard to either holy war or slavery, but solely in regard to polygamy and divorce*—this is because it derives from a different aspect of the total Truth. Christianity, like Buddhism, considers only the carnal side of sexuality, therefore its substantial or quantitative aspect. Islam, on the other hand, like Judaism and the Hindu and Chinese religions—apart from certain spiritual ways that reject sexual love for reasons of method—considers the essential or qualitative aspect of sexuality, or what we might call its cosmic aspect; and in fact the sanctification of sexuality confers upon it a quality that transcends its carnal aspect and neutralizes or even abolishes the latter in certain cases, for instance, in the case of the Cassandras and Sybils of antiquity or of the tantric *Shrī Chakra,* or lastly, in that of great spiritual figures such as Solomon and Mohammed. In other words, sexuality can have a noble aspect, just as it can have one that is impure. To speak in terms of geometric symbolism it may be considered

* Polygamy was necessary for the peoples of the Middle East—who are warrior peoples—to ensure that all the women should be provided for notwithstanding the killing off of the men in the wars; a further reason was the high rate of mortality among infants, which made polygamy virtually necessary for the preservation of the race. As for divorce, it was, and is, made necessary by the inevitable separation of the sexes, which results in the bride and bridegroom not knowing one another, or hardly knowing one another, before marriage; this separation is itself made necessary by the sensual temperament of the Arabs and of southern peoples in general. What has just been said explains the wearing of the veil by Moslem women and also the *pardah* of high-caste Hindu women. The fact that the veil is worn only in the latest religious form, namely Islam, and that the *pardah* is a comparatively recent introduction into Hinduism, shows that the need for these measures arises out of conditions that are particular to the end of the Iron Age. It is owing to the existence of these same conditions that women have been excluded from certain Brahmanic rites to which they formerly had access.

in a vertical as well as a horizontal sense; the flesh is impure in itself, with or without sexuality, and the latter is noble in itself, in or out of the flesh. This nobility of sexuality derives from its Divine Prototype, for "God is Love." In Islamic terms one would say that "God is Unity," and that love, being a mode of union (*tawḥīd*), is for that reason a way of conforming to the Divine Nature. Love can sanctify the flesh, just as the flesh can debase love. Islam insists on the first of these truths, while Christianity tends to insist on the second, except of course in the sacrament of marriage, in which it unavoidably and as it were incidentally rejoins the Judaeo-Islamic perspective.

3

Our next task is to show wherein really lies the difference between the respective manifestations of Christ and Mohammed. It must, however, be emphasized that differences of this kind concern only the manifestation of "God-men" and not their inward and Divine reality, which is identical. Meister Eckhart has expressed this identity in the following terms: "Everything that the Holy Scriptures say about Christ is equally true of every good and divine man," that is to say, of every man who possesses the plenitude of spiritual realization, both in the sense of breadth and of height. Again, Shrī Ramakrishna says: "In the Absolute I am not, and thou art not, and God is not, for It is beyond speech and thought. But so long as anything exists outside myself, I ought to adore Brahma, within the limits of the mind, as something existing outside myself"; this explains, on the one hand, how it was that Christ could pray, though being himself Divine, and on the other hand, how it was possible for the Prophet, while unmistakably man by reason of the particular mode of his manifestation, to be at the same time Divine in his inward reality. In the same order of ideas, we would also point out that the exoteric perspective is based essentially upon a fact to which it attributes a character of absoluteness. For example, the Christian perspective is based on the supreme spiritual state realized by Christ, but it attributes this state to Christ alone, whence the denial, at least in ordinary theology, of metaphysical Deliverance or the Beatific Vision in this life. It should be added that esoterism, speaking through the voice of Meister Eckhart, brings back the mystery of the Incarnation within the sphere of spiritual laws when it attributes to the man who has attained the highest sanctity all the characteristics of Christ with the exception of the Prophetic, or rather, redemptive, mission. An analogous example is provided by the claim made by several Sufis that certain of their writings are on the same level of inspiration as the Koran. In exoteric Islam, this degree of inspiration is attributed to the Prophet alone, in conformity with the theological perspective that is always founded on a transcendent fact appropriated exclusively on behalf of a particular manifestation of the Word.

We have previously mentioned the fact that it is the Koran that in all strictness corresponds to the Christ-Eucharist, and that represents the great Paracletic manifestation, a "descent" (*tanzīl*) effectuated by the Holy Spirit (*Ar-Rūḥ,* called *Jibrīl*—Gabriel—in its function as Revealer). It follows that the function of the Prophet is from this point of view analogous and symbolically even identical to that of the Blessed Virgin, who was likewise the "ground" for the reception of the Word. Just as the Blessed Virgin, fecundated by the Holy Ghost, is "Co-Redemptress" and "Queen of Heaven," created before the rest of the Creation, so the Prophet, inspired by the same Paracletic Spirit, is "Messenger of Mercy" (*Rasūl ar-Raḥmah*) and "Lord of the Two Existences" (this world and the next) (*Sayyid al-Kawnayn*), and was likewise created before all other beings. This priority of creation signifies that the Virgin and the Prophet incarnate a principial or metacosmic Reality;* they are

---

* The opinion that Christ was the *Mleccha Avatāra,* the "Divine Descent of the Barbarians" (or "for the Barbarians"), that is to say, the ninth incarnation of Vishnu, must be rejected for reasons both of traditional fact and of principle. In the first place the Buddha ħas always been considered by Hindus as an *Avatāra,* though since Hinduism had necessarily to exclude Buddhism, the apparent Buddhist heresy was explained, on the one hand, by the need to abolish blood sacrifices, and on the other hand, by the need to involve corrupted men in error in order to hasten the inevitable advance of the *Kali-yuga.* In the second place, it is impossible that a being having an organic place in the Hindu system should belong to a world other than India, particularly one as remote as the Judaic world.

identified—in their receptive function, though not in their Divine Knowledge, nor, in the case of Mohammed, in his Prophetic function—with the passive aspect of universal Existence (*Prakriti;* in Arabic, *al-Lawḥ al-Maḥfūz,* "the Guarded Tablet"), and it is for this reason that the Virgin is "immaculate" and, from the merely physical standpoint, "virgin," while the Prophet, like the Apostles, is "illiterate" (*ummī*), that is to say, pure from the taint of human knowledge or knowledge humanly acquired. This purity is the first condition for the reception of the Paracletic Gift, just as in the spiritual order chastity, poverty, humility, and other forms of simplicity or unity are indispensable for the reception of the Divine Light. As a further illustration of this analogical relationship between the Virgin and the Prophet, it may be added that the particular state in which the Prophet was immersed at the time of the Revelations is directly comparable to that of the Virgin when carrying or giving birth to the Child Jesus. However by reason of his Prophetic function, in the highest meaning of the term, Mohammed is also more than the Virgin, and when he utters the Koranic suras, or more generally whenever the "Divine Ego" speaks through his mouth, he is directly identified with the Christ, who is Himself what the Revelation is for the Prophet and whose every word is consequently Divine Speech. In the case of the Prophet, only the "words of the Most Holy" (*aḥādīth qudsīyah*) possess, apart from the Koran, this Divine character; his other words proceed from a subordinate degree of inspiration (*nafas ar-Rūḥ;* the Hindu *smriti*), as do also certain parts of the New Testament, in particular the Epistles. To return to the purity of the Prophet, we also find in his case the exact equivalent of the "Immaculate Conception"; according to the traditional account two angels cleft open the chest of the infant Mohammed and with snow cleansed him of "original sin," which appeared in the form of a black stain on his heart. Mohammed, like Mary and the human nature of Jesus, is not therefore an ordinary man, and it is for this reason that it is said that "Mohammed is [simply] a man, not as [ordinary] men are, but in the manner of a jewel among [common] stones" (*Muḥammadun basharun lā ka-'l-bashari bal huwa ka-'l-yāqūti bayna* 'l-ḥajar). This brings to mind the formula of the Ave Maria, "Blessed art thou among women," which indicates that the Virgin, in herself and apart from her reception of the Holy Ghost, is a "jewel" compared with other creatures, thus, as it were, a "sublime norm."

In a certain respect the Virgin and the Prophet incarnate the passive or feminine aspect—or pole—of universal Existence (*Prakriti*); they therefore incarnate *a fortiori* the beneficent and merciful aspect of *Prakriti,* namely Lakshmi (the Kwan Yin of the Far Eastern Tradition), and this explains their essential function as intercessors, and accounts for names such as "Mother of Mercy" (*Mater Misericordiae*) and "Our Lady of Perpetual Help" (*Nostra Domina a perpetuo succursu*), as well as the names given to the Prophet such as "Key to God's Mercy" (*Miftāḥ Raḥmat Allāh*), "Merciful" (*Raḥīm*), "Healer" (*Shāfī*), "Remover of Grief" (*Kāshif al-Kurab*), "Effacer of Sins" (*'Afūw*), and "Most Beautiful Creation of God" (*Ajmal Khalq Allāh*). If it be asked what relationship exists between this mercy, this pardon, or this beneficence and universal Existence, we would reply as follows: since Existence is undifferentiated, virgin, or pure in relation to its productions, it is able to reabsorb in its undifferentiation the differentiated qualities of things; in other words, the disequilibriums of manifestation are always capable of being integrated in the principial equilibrium. Now all evil comes from a cosmic quality (guna), hence from a rupture of equilibrium, and since Existence carries all the qualities within itself in undifferentiated equilibrium, it is capable of dissolving in its infinity all the vicissitudes of the world. Existence is in reality both "Virgin" and "Mother," in the sense that, on the one hand, it is determined by nothing apart from God, and on the other hand, it gives birth to the manifested Universe. Mary is "Virgin Mother" by reason of the mystery of the Incarnation; as for Mohammed, he is, as we have seen, "virgin" or "illiterate" insofar as he is inspired only by God and receives nothing from men, and he is "Mother" by reason of his power of intercession with God; the personifications of the Divine *Prakriti,* whether human or angelic, essentially reveal the aspects of purity and love.

The aspect of Grace or Mercy belonging to the "virginal" and "maternal" Divinity also explains why the latter readily manifests itself in a sensible form and in human guise, thereby becoming accessible to men: the apparitions of the Virgin are well known in the West, and in the case of the Prophet his apparitions to pious Moslems are not infrequent; there even exist methods for obtaining this grace, which is equivalent in reality to a concretization of the Beatific Vision.*

Although the Prophet does not occupy in Islam the same place that Christ occupies in Christianity, he nevertheless of necessity enjoys a central position in the Islamic perspective. It remains for us to make clear by virtue of what truth this can and must be so, and further to show how Islam integrates Christ in its perspective while at the same time recognizing his solar nature, as it were on the basis of his virgin birth. According to this perspective, the Word does not manifest itself in any particular man as such, but in the Prophetic function—in the highest sense of the term—and above all, in the revealed Books; and since the Prophetic function of Mohammed is real and the Koran a true Revelation, Moslems, who admit only these two criteria, see no reason for placing Jesus before Mohammed. Indeed they must give precedence to Mohammed, inasmuch as the latter, being the last representative of the Prophetic function, recapitulates and synthesizes every aspect of this function and closes the cycle of manifestation of the Word, whence the title "Seal of the Prophets" (*Khātam al-anbiyā'*). It is this unique situation that confers upon Mohammed the central position that he enjoys in Islam and that allows of the Word itself being named "Mohammedan Light" (*Nūr Muhammadī*).

The fact that the Islamic perspective is concerned only with Revelation as such, and not with all its possible modes, explains why Islam does not attach the same importance as Christianity to

* In this connection we may also recall the apparitions of the Shakti in Hinduism—for example to Shrī Ramakrishna and Shrī Sarada Devi—and those of Kwan Yin or Kwannon in the religions of the Far East, for example, to Shinran Shōnin, the great Japanese Buddhist saint; it is also known that in Judaism the *Shekhīnah* appears in the form of a beautiful and gracious woman.

the miracles of Christ. In fact all the Messengers, including Mohammed, have performed miracles (*mu'jizāt*);* the difference in this respect between Christ and the other Messengers is that only in the case of Christ does the miracle possess a central importance, being wrought by God "in" the human support and not merely "through" this support. This part played by the miracle in Christianity is explained by the particular features that constitute the reason for the existence of this form of Revelation, the nature of which will be examined in the following chapter. From the Islamic point of view it is not the miracles that matter so much as the Divine nature of the Messenger's mission, irrespective of how important miracles may be in that mission. It might be said that the particularity of Christianity consists in the fact that it is based first and foremost on a miracle, which is perpetuated in the Eucharist, whereas Islam is essentially based on an Idea, supported by human means, though with Divine aid, and perpetuated in the Koranic Revelation of which the ritual prayer is as it were a ceaselessly renewed actualization.

We have already mentioned that in his inner reality, Mohammed, like Christ, is identified with the Word, as indeed is every being who has achieved metaphysical realization in its fullness;† whence the following *ahādīth:* "He who has seen me has seen God [under His aspect of absolute Truth]" (*Man ra'ānī fa-qad rā'a 'l-*

* The majority of Orientalists, if not all, falsely deduce from various passages in the Koran that the Prophet accomplished no miracles, a deduction that is contradicted in advance, not only by the traditional commentators of the Koran, but also by the *Sunnah,* which is the pillar of Islamic orthodoxy.

With regard to the "avataric" nature of the Prophet, without mentioning infallible criteria of a more profound order, it is witnessed by the signs that, according to the *Sunnah,* preceded and accompanied his birth, signs that are analogous to those associated with Christ and Buddha in the Christian and Buddhist religions.

† This metaphysical realization, which integrates man in his Divine Prototype, so that one may say of the being possessing this supreme state that "he is not created" (*Aṣ-Ṣūfī lam yukhlaq*), is within hardly anybody's reach in our cyclic period; if we speak of it nevertheless, it is solely out of regard for doctrinal truth, for without the idea of the "God-man," esoterism would be deprived of an aspect of its very essence.

Ḥaqq), and "He [Mohammed] was Prophet [Word] when **Adam** was still between water and mud" (*Fa-kāna nabīyan wa-'Adamu bayna 'l-mā'i wa-'ṭ-ṭīn*), words that can be compared with these words of Christ: "I and my Father are one," and "Verily I say unto you, before Abraham was, I am."

Universality and Particular Nature of the Christian Religion

1

What, for want of a better term, we have been obliged to call "Christian exoterism" is not, in its origin and structure, strictly analogous to the Judaic and Islamic exoterisms; for whereas the exoteric side of the two latter religions was instituted as such from the very beginning, in the sense that it formed part of the Revelation and was clearly distinguishable from its esoteric aspect, what we now know as Christian exoterism hardly figured as such in the Christian Revelation except in a purely incidental manner. It is true that in the oldest texts, particularly in the Epistles of Saint Paul, there are suggestions of a point of view that may be called exoteric. Such is the case, for example, when the principal hierarchic connection existing between esoterism and exoterism is represented in the guise of a sort of historical relationship between the New Covenant and the Old, the former being identified with the "spirit that giveth life" and the latter with the "letter that killeth,"* a comparison that leaves out of account the integral reality inherent in the Old Covenant itself, namely, that element in it that is identified principally with the New Covenant, and of

---

* The interpretation of these words in an exoteric sense is really an act of suicide, for they are bound inevitably to turn against the exoterism that has annexed them. The truth of this was demonstrated by the Reformation, which eagerly seized upon the phrase in question (2 Cor. 3:6) in order to make of it its chief weapon, thus usurping the place that normally should belong to esoterism.

which the latter is simply a new form or adaptation. This is a good example of how the exoteric or theological point of view,* instead of embracing a truth in its entirety, selects one aspect only as a matter of expediency and gives it an exclusive and absolute value; it should not be forgotten, however, that but for this dogmatic character religious truth would be inefficacious with regard to the particular end imposed upon it by the motives of expediency already mentioned. There is thus a twofold restriction put upon pure truth: on the one hand, an aspect of the truth is invested with the character of integral truth; and on the other hand, an absolute character is attributed to the relative. Furthermore, this standpoint of expediency carries with it the negation of all those things that, being neither accessible nor indispensable to everyone indiscriminately, lie for that reason beyond the aim of the theological perspective and must be left outside it—hence the simplifications and symbolical syntheses peculiar to every exoterism.† Lastly, we may

* Christianity inherited this point of view from Judaism, whose form coincides with the origin of this perspective; it is almost superfluous to stress the fact that its presence in primitive Christianity in no wise invalidates the initiatory essence of the latter. "There exist," says Origen, "diverse forms of the Word under which It reveals Itself to Its disciples, conforming Itself to the degree of light of each one, according to the degree of their progress in holiness" (*Contra Cels.* 4:16).

† Thus, Semitic exoterism denies the transmigration of the soul and consequently the existence of an immortal soul in animals; and it also denies the total cyclic dissolution that the Hindus call *mahā-pralaya,* a dissolution that implies the annihilation of the entire Creation (*samsāra*). These truths are in nowise indispensable for salvation, and even involve certain dangers for the mentalities to which these are addressed; in other words, an exoterism is always obliged to pass over in silence any esoteric elements that are incompatible with its own dogmatic form, or even to deny them.

However, in order to forestall possible objections to the examples just given, two reservations need to be made. In the first place, with regard to the immortality of the soul in the case of animals, it should be said that the theological denial is justified in the sense that a being cannot in fact attain immortality while bound to the animal state, since the latter, like the vegetable and mineral states, is peripheral, and immortality and deliverance can be attained only from the starting point of a central state such as the human one. It will be seen from this example that a religious negation that is dogmatic in character is never meaningless. In the second place, with regard to the refusal to admit the *mahā-pralaya,* it should be added that this negation is not strictly dogmatic and that the total cyclic dissolution, which

also mention, as a particularly striking feature of these doctrines, the identification of historical facts with principal truths and the inevitable confusions resulting therefrom. For example, when it is said that all human souls, from that of Adam to the departed souls of Christ's own contemporaries, had to await His descent into Hell in order to be delivered, such a statement confuses the historical with the cosmic Christ and represents an eternal function of the Word as a temporal fact, for the simple reason that Jesus was a manifestation of this Word; which is another way of saying that in the world where this manifestation took place, Jesus was truly the unique incarnation of the Word. Another example may be found in the divergent views of Christianity and Islam on the subject of the death of Christ: apart from the fact that the Koran, by its apparent denial of Christ's death, is simply affirming that Christ was not killed in reality—which is obvious not only as regards the Divine nature of the God-man, but also as regards His human nature, since it was resurrected—the refusal of Moslems to admit the historical Redemption, and consequently the facts that are the unique terrestrial expression of Universal Redemption as far as Christian humanity is concerned, simply denotes that in the final analysis Christ did not die for those who are "whole," who in this case are the Moslems insofar as they benefit from another terrestrial form of the One and Eternal Redemption. In other words, if it be true in principle that Christ died for all men—in the same way that the Islamic Revelation is principially addressed to everyone—in fact He died only for those who must and do benefit from the means of grace that perpetuate His work of Redemption;* hence

---

completes a "life of Brahmā," is clearly attested by scriptural passages such as the following: "For verily I say unto you, till heaven and earth pass, one jot or one tittle shall in no wise pass from the law, till all be fulfilled" (Matt. 5:18); "They shall remain there [khālidīn] for as long as the heavens and the earth endure, unless thy Lord willeth otherwise" (Koran 11:107).

* In the same order of ideas, the following words of Saint Augustine may be cited: "That which today is called the Christian religion existed among the Ancients and has never ceased to exist from the origin of the human race until the time when Christ Himself came and men began to call Christian the true religion which already existed beforehand" (Retract. I, 13. 3). This passage has been commented upon as follows by the Abbé P.-J. Jallabert in his book Le Catholicisme avant Jésus-Christ: "The Catholic religion is but a

the traditional distance separating Islam from the Christian Mystery is bound, outwardly at least, to appear in the form of a denial, exactly in the same way that Christian exoterism must deny the possibility of salvation outside the Redemption wrought by Jesus. However that may be, although a religious perspective may be contested *ad extra,* that is to say, in the light of another religious perspective deriving from a different aspect of the same truth, it remains incontestable *ad intra,* inasmuch as its capacity to serve as a means of expressing the total truth makes of it a key to the latter. Moreover it must never be forgotten that the restrictions inherent in the dogmatic point of view express in their own way the Divine Goodness that wishes to prevent men from going astray, and that gives them what is accessible and indispensable to everyone, having regard to the mental predispositions of the human collectivity concerned.*

It will be understood from what has just been said that any seeming contradiction or depreciation of the Mosaic Law that may be found in the words of Christ or the teaching of the Apostles is in reality but an expression of the superiority of esoterism over exoterism† and does not therefore apply at the same level as this

---

continuation of the primitive religion restored and generously enriched by Him Who knew His work from the beginning. This explains why St. Paul the Apostle did not claim to be superior to the Gentiles save in his knowledge of Jesus crucified. In fact, all the Gentiles needed to acquire was the knowledge of the Incarnation and the Redemption considered as an accomplished fact; for they had already received the deposit of all the remaining truths. . . . It is well to consider that this Divine Revelation, which idolatry had rendered unrecognizable, had nevertheless been preserved in its purity and perhaps in all its perfection in the mysteries of Eleusis, Lemnos, and Samothrace." This "knowledge of the Incarnation and the Redemption" implies before all else a knowledge of the renewal effected by Christ of a means of grace that in itself is eternal, like the Law that Christ came to fulfill but not to destroy. This means of grace is essentially always the same and the only means that exists, however its modes may vary in accordance with the different ethnic and cultural environments to which it reveals itself; the Eucharist is a universal reality like Christ Himself.

* In an analogous sense it is said in Islam that "the divergence of the exegetists is a blessing" (*Ikhtilāf al-'ulamā' raḥmah*).

† This is brought out in a particularly clear manner by the words of Christ concerning St. John the Baptist. From the exoteric point of view it is obvious that the Prophet who stands nearest to the Christ-God is the

Law,* at least not a priori, that is to say so long as this hierarchic relationship is not itself conceived in an exoteric mode. It is perfectly obvious that the main teachings of Christ transcend the exoteric viewpoint, and that is indeed the reason for their existence. They therefore likewise transcend the Law; in no other way could one explain the attitude of Christ with respect to the lex talionis, or with regard to the woman taken in adultery, or to divorce. In fact the turning of the other cheek is not a thing that any social collectivity could put into practice with a view to maintaining its equilibrium,† and it has no meaning except as a spiritual attitude;

---

greatest among men, and on the other hand, that the least among the Blessed in Heaven is greater than the greatest man on earth, always by reason of this same proximity to God. Metaphysically, the words of Christ express the superiority of what is principial over what is manifested, or from an initiatory point of view, of esoterism over exoterism, St. John the Baptist being in this case regarded as the summit and fulfillment of the latter, which explains furthermore why his name is identical with that of St. John the Evangelist, who represents Christianity in its most inward aspect.

* In St. Paul's epistle to the Romans, one finds the following passage: "For circumcision verily profiteth, if thou keep the law: but if thou be a breaker of the law, thy circumcision is made uncircumcision. Therefore if the uncircumcision keep the righteousness of the law, shall not his uncircumcision be counted for circumcision? And shall not uncircumcision which is by nature, if it fulfill the law, judge thee, who by the letter and circumcision dost transgress the law? For he is not a Jew, which is one outwardly; neither is that circumcision, which is outward in the flesh; but he is a Jew, which is one inwardly; and circumcision is that of the heart, in the spirit, and not in the letter; whose praise is not of men but of God." (Rom. 2:25–29)

The same idea reappears, in a more concise form, in the following passage from the Koran: "And they say: Become Jews or Nazarenes in order that you may be guided; answer: No, we follow the way of Abraham who was pure [or "primordial," *ḥanīf*] and who was not one of those who associate [creatures with Allāh, or effects with the Cause, or manifestations with the Principle]. [Receive] the baptism of Allāh [and not that of men]; and who indeed baptises better than Allāh? and it is Him whom we adore" [*Sūrat al-Baqarah* 135, 138]. The "baptism" referred to here expresses the same fundamental idea that St. Paul expresses by the word "circumcision."

† This is so clearly true that Christians themselves have never turned this injunction of Christ into a legal obligation, which proves once again that it is not situated on the same level as the Judaic Law and consequently was neither intended nor able to take its place.

There is a *ḥadīth* that shows the compatibility existing between the spiritual point of view affirmed by Christ and the social point of view that is that of the Mosaic Law. It is related that the first thief among the Moslem

the spiritual man alone firmly takes his stand outside the logical chain of individual reactions, since for him a participation in the current of these reactions is tantamount to a fall from grace, at least when such participation involves the center or the soul of the individual, though not when it remains purely an outward and impersonal act of justice such as that envisaged by the Mosaic Law. But it was precisely because this impersonal character of the lex talionis had been lost and replaced by passions that it was needful for Christ to express a spiritual truth that, although only condemning a false pretension, appeared to condemn the Law itself. All this is clearly evidenced in Christ's answer to those who wished to stone the woman taken in adultery, and who, instead of acting impersonally in the name of the Law, would have acted personally in the name of their own hypocrisy. Christ did not therefore speak from the standpoint of the Law, but from that of inward, suprasocial and spiritual realities; and His point of view was exactly the same on the question of divorce. Perhaps the most striking proof to be found in Christ's teachings of the purely spiritual and therefore suprasocial and extramoral character of His Doctrine, is contained in the following saying: "If any man come to me and hate not his father, and mother, and wife and children and brethren and sisters, yea, and his own life also, he cannot be my disciple" (Luke 14:26). It is clearly impossible to oppose such teaching to the Mosaic Law.

Christianity accordingly possesses none of the normal characteristics of an exoterism instituted as such, but presents itself as an exoterism in fact rather than one existing in principle. Moreover, even without referring to Scriptural passages, the essentially initiatory character of Christianity is apparent from certain features of the first importance, such as the Doctrine of the Trinity, the

---

community was led before the Prophet in order that his hand might be cut off according to the Koranic law, but the Prophet turned pale. He was asked: "Hast thou some objection?" He answered: "How should I have nothing to object to! Must I be the ally of Satan in enmity against my brothers? If you wish God to forgive your sin and conceal it, you also must conceal the sin of others. For once the transgressor has been brought before the monarch, the punishment must be executed."

Sacrament of the Eucharist, and more particularly, the use of wine in this rite, or again, from the use of purely esoteric expressions such as "Son of God" and especially "Mother of God." If exoterism is "something that is at the same time indispensable and accessible to all,"* Christianity cannot be exoteric in the usual sense of the word, since it is in reality by no means accessible to everyone, although in fact, by virtue of its outward application, it is binding upon everyone. This inaccessibility of the Christian dogmas is expressed by calling them "mysteries," a word that has a positive meaning only in the initiatory domain to which moreover it belongs, but which, when applied in the theological sphere, seems to attempt to justify or conceal the fact that Christian dogmas carry with them no direct intellectual proof. For example, the Divine Unity is a truth that is immediately evident and therefore capable of exoteric or dogmatic formulation, for this idea, in its simplest expression, is one that is accessible to every man whose mind is sound; on the other hand, the Trinity, inasmuch as it corresponds to a more differentiated point of view and represents a particular development of the Doctrine of Unity among others that are equally possible, is not strictly speaking capable of exoteric formulation, for the simple reason that a differentiated or derived metaphysical conception is not accessible to everyone. Moreover, the Trinity necessarily corresponds to a more relative point of view than that of Unity, in the same way that Redemption is a reality more relative than Creation. Any normal man can to a certain extent conceive the Divine Unity, because this is the most universal, and therefore in a certain sense the most simple, aspect of the Divinity; on the other hand, the Trinity can only be understood by those who are capable of conceiving the Divinity under other more or less relative aspects, that is to say, by those who are able, through spiritual participation in the Divine Intellect, to move, as it were, in the metaphysical dimension; but that, precisely, is a possibility that is very far from being accessible to everyone, at least in the present state of humanity. When Saint Augustine said that the Trinity was incomprehensible, he was necessarily speaking—

* Definition given by René Guénon in his article "Création et Manifestation" (*Études Traditionnelles,* October, 1937).

doubtless in conformity with the tendencies of the Roman world—from the rational point of view of the individual, a point of view that when applied to transcendent truths, can but reveal its own inadequacy. The only thing that is completely incomprehensible, from the standpoint of pure intellectuality, is that which is totally unreal, in other words, pure nothingness, which is the same thing as impossibility, and which, being nothing, cannot become an object of understanding.

Let it be added that the esoteric nature of the Christian dogmas and sacraments is the underlying cause of the Islamic reaction against Christianity. Because the latter had mixed together the *Ḥaqīqah* (the esoteric Truth and the *Sharīʿah* (the exoteric Law), it carried with it certain dangers of disequilibrium that have in fact manifested themselves during the course of the centuries, indirectly contributing to the terrible subversion represented by the modern world, in conformity with the words of Christ: "Give not that which is holy unto the dogs, neither cast ye your pearls before swine, lest they trample them under their feet, and turn again and rend you."

2

Now if Christianity seems to confuse two domains that should normally remain separate, just as it confuses the two Eucharistic species that respectively represent these domains, it may be asked whether things might have been otherwise and whether this confusion is simply the result of individual errors. Assuredly not and for the following reasons. The inward and esoteric truth must of necessity sometimes manifest itself in broad daylight, this being by virtue of a definite possibility of spiritual manifestation and without regard to the shortcomings of a particular human environment; in other words, the confusion in question* is but the negative con-

* The most general example of this confusion, which might also be called a fluctuation, is the mingling in the Scriptures of the New Testament of the two degrees of inspiration that Hindus denote respectively by the terms *shruti* and *smriti,* and Moslems by the terms *nafas ar-Rūḥ* and *ilqā ar-*

sequence of something that in itself is positive, namely, the manifestation of Christ as such. It is to this manifestation as well as to all other analogous manifestations of the Word, whatever their degree of universality, that the following inspired words relate: "And the Light shineth in darkness, and the darkness comprehendeth it not." It was necessary that Christ, by metaphysical or cosmological definition as it were, should break the husk represented by the Mosaic Law, though without denying the latter; being Himself the living kernel of this Law, He had every right to do so, for He was "more true" than it, and this is one of the meanings of His words, "Before Abraham was, I am." It may also be said that if esoterism does not concern everyone, it is for the reason, analogically speaking, that light penetrates some substances and not others; but on the other hand, if esoterism must manifest itself openly from time to time, as happened in the case of Christ, and, at a lower level of universality, in the case of Al-Ḥallāj, it is, still by analogy, because the sun illuminates everything without distinction. Thus, if the "Light shineth in darkness," in the principial or universal sense we are concerned with here, this is because in so doing it manifests one of its possibilities, and a possibility, by definition, is something that cannot not be, being an aspect of the absolute necessity of the Divine Principle.

These considerations must not lead us to overlook a complementary though more contingent aspect of the question. There must also exist on the human side, that is to say, in the environment in which such a Divine manifestation takes place, a sufficient reason for its occurrence; so, for the world to which Christ's mission was addressed, this open manifestation of truths that should normally remain hidden—under certain conditions of time and place at least—was the only possible means of bringing about the reorientation of which that world had need. This is sufficient to

---

Raḥmānīyah: the latter expression, like the word *smriti,* denotes a derived or secondary inspiration, while the first expression, like the word *shruti,* refers to Revelation properly so-called, that is to say, to the Divine Word in a direct sense. In the Epistles, this mingling even appears explicitly on several occasions; the seventh chapter of the First Epistle to the Corinthians is particularly instructive in this respect.

justify that element in the spiritual radiation of Christ that would be abnormal and illegitimate under ordinary circumstances. This laying bare of the "spirit" hidden in the "letter" could not, however, entirely do away with certain laws that are inherent in all esoterism, under pain of changing the nature of the latter entirely: thus Christ spoke only in parables, "that it might be fulfilled which was spoken by the Prophet, saying, I will open my mouth in parables; I will utter things which have been kept secret from the foundation of the world" (Matt. 13:34, 35). Nonetheless, a radiation of this kind, though inevitable in the particular case in question, constitutes as it were a "two-edged sword." But there is another thing to be considered, namely, that the Christian way is essentially a way of Grace, being in this respect analogous to the "bhaktic" ways of India and certain ways to be found in Buddhism. In methods like these, by reason of their very nature, the distinction between an outer and an inner aspect is attenuated, in the sense that Grace, which is initiatory in its kernel or essence, tends to bestow itself in the largest measure possible, which it is enabled to do by virtue of the simplicity and universality of the symbolism and means proper to it. It may also be said that while the difference separating the way of merit from the way of Knowledge is of necessity very great, in view of the fact that these two ways refer respectively to meritorious action and intellectual contemplation, the way of Grace occupies in a certain sense a position midway between the two. Thus, in the way of Grace the inward and outward applications go hand in hand in the same radiation of Mercy, while in the sphere of spiritual realization the differences will be of degree rather than of principle; every intelligence and every will is able to participate in one and the same Grace according to the measure of its possibilities, and this recalls the image of the sun illuminating everything without distinction, while acting differently on different substances.

Now apart from the fact that a synthetic mode of radiation such as that just described—with its laying bare of things that a normal exoterism will leave veiled—was the only possible way to give effect to the spiritual reorientation of which the Western world stood in need, it must be added that this mode also possesses a providential aspect in relation to cyclic evolution, in the sense of being a part of the Divine Plan concerning the final development of the present cycle of humanity. From another point of view one may also recognize, in the disproportion between the purely spiritual quality of the Gift of Christ and the heterogeneous nature of the environment into which it was received, the mark of an exceptional mode of Divine Mercy, which constantly renews itself for the sake of creatures: in order to save one of the "sick" parts of humanity, or rather "a humanity," God consents to be profaned; but on the other hand—and this is a manifestation of His Impersonality, which by definition lies beyond the exoteric point of view —He makes use of this profanation, since "it must needs be that offences come," in order to bring about the final decadence of the present cycle of humanity, this decadence being necessary for the exhausting of all the possibilities included in this cycle, necessary therefore for the equilibrium of the cycle as a whole and the fulfillment of the glorious and universal radiation of God.

The exoteric point of view is compelled, under penalty of having to admit that the actions of its Personal God, the only one it takes into consideration, contradict one another, to define the apparently contradictory acts of the Impersonal Divinity—when it cannot deny them purely and simply as it does in the case of the diversity of religious forms—as "mysterious" and "unfathomable," while naturally attributing these "mysteries" to the Will of the Personal God.

3

The existence of a Christian esoterism, or rather the eminently esoteric character of primitive Christianity, does not appear only from New Testament texts—those in which certain of Christ's words possess no exoteric meaning—or from the nature of the Christian rites—to mention only what is, so to speak, accessible "from without" in the Latin Church—but also from the explicit testimony of the older authors. Thus, in his work on the Holy Ghost St. Basil speaks of a tacit and mystical tradition maintained down to our own times, and of a secret instruction that our fathers observed without discussion and which we follow by dwelling in the simplicity of their silence. For they understood how necessary was silence in order to maintain the respect and veneration due to our Holy Mysteries. And in fact it was not expedient to make known in writing a doctrine containing things that catechumens are not permitted to contemplate.

Again, according to St. Denys the Areopagite,

Salvation is possible only for deified souls, and deification is nothing else but the union and resemblance we strive to have with God. That which is bestowed uniformly and all at once, so to speak, on the Blessed Essences dwelling in Heaven, is transmitted to us as it were in fragments and through the multiplicity of the varied symbols of the Divine oracles. For it is on these Divine oracles that our hierarchy is founded. And by these words we mean not only what our inspired Masters have left us in the Holy Epistles and in their theological works, but also what they transmitted to their disciples by a kind of spiritual and almost heavenly teaching, initiating them from person to person in a bodily way no doubt, since they spoke, but I venture to say, in an immaterial way also, since they did not write. But since these truths had to be translated into the usages of the Church, the Apostles expressed them under the veil of symbols and not in their sublime nakedness, for not everyone is holy, and as the Scriptures say, Knowledge is not for all.[1]

4

We have seen that Christianity is a way of Grace or of Love (the *bhakti-marga* of the Hindus), and this definition calls for some further explanation of a general kind. The most pronounced difference between the New Covenant and the Old is that in the latter the Divine Aspect of Justice predominated, whereas in the former it is, on the contrary, the Aspect of Mercy that prevails. The way of Mercy is, in a certain sense, easier than the way of Justice because, while corresponding at the same time to a more profound reality, it also benefits from a special Grace: this is the "justification by Faith" whose "yoke is easy and burden light," and which renders the "yoke of Heaven" of the Mosaic Law unnecessary. Moreover, this "justification by Faith" is analogous—and its whole esoteric significance rests on this—to "liberation by Knowledge," both being to a greater or less extent independent of the Law, that is to say, of works.[2] Faith is in fact nothing else than the "bhaktic" mode of Knowledge and of intellectual certainty, which means that Faith is a passive act of the intelligence, its immediate object being not the truth as such, but a symbol of the truth. This symbol will yield up its secrets in proportion to the greatness of the Faith, which in its turn will be determined by an attitude of confidence or of emotional certainty, that is to say, by an element of bhakti, or Love. Insofar as Faith is a contemplative attitude, its subject is the intelligence; it can therefore be said to constitute a virtual Knowledge; but since its mode is passive, it must compensate this passivity by a complementary active attitude, that is to say, by an attitude of the will the substance of which is precisely confidence and fervor, by virtue of which the intelligence will receive spiritual certainties. Faith is a priori a natural disposition of the soul to admit the supernatural; it is therefore essentially an intuition of the supernatural, brought about by Grace, which is actualized by means of the attitude of fervent confidence.* When,

---

* The life of the great *bhakta* Shrī Ramakrishna provides a very instructive example of the "bhaktic" mode of knowledge. The saint wished to understand the identity between gold and clay; but instead of starting out from a metaphysical datum that would have enabled him to perceive the vanity of riches, as a *jnānin* would have done, he kept praying to Kālī to cause him to understand this identity by a revelation:

. . . every morning, for many long months, I held in my hand a piece of money and a lump of clay and repeated: *gold is clay and clay is gold*. But this thought brought no spiritual work into operation within me; nothing came to prove to me the truth of such a statement. After I know not how many months of meditation, I was sitting one morning at dawn on the bank of the river, imploring our Mother to enlighten me. All of a sudden the whole universe appeared before my eyes clothed in a sparkling mantle of gold. . . . Then the landscape took on a duller glow, the colour of brown clay, even lovelier than the gold. And while this vision engraved itself deeply on my soul, I heard a sound like the trumpeting of more than ten thousand elephants who clamoured in my ear: *Clay and gold are but one thing for you*. My prayers were answered, and I threw far away into the Ganges the piece of gold and the lump of clay. [Romain Rolland, *La vie de Ramakrishna*]

In the same connection, the following reflections of an orthodox theologian may be quoted: "A dogma that expresses a revealed truth, which

through Grace, Faith becomes complete, it will have been dissolved in Love, which is God; that is why, from the theological standpoint, the blessed in Heaven no longer have Faith, since they behold its object, namely, God, who is Love or Beatitude. It should be added that from an initiatory point of view, as expressed for example in the teaching of the Hesychast tradition, this vision can and even should be obtained in this life. Another aspect of Faith that may be mentioned here is the connection between Faith and miracles, a connection that explains the great importance of miracles not only in the case of Christ, but in Christianity as such. In Christianity, by contrast with Islam, the miracle plays a central and quasi-organic part, and this is not unconnected with the "bhaktic" nature of the Christian way. Miracles would in fact be inexplicable apart from the role they play in Faith; possessing no persuasive value in themselves—for otherwise satanic miracles would be a criterion of truth—they nevertheless possess this value to an extreme degree in association with all the other factors that enter into the Christian Revelation. In other words, if the miracles of Christ, the Apostles, and the Saints are precious and venerable, this is solely because they are associated with other criteria that a priori permit of their being invested with the value of Divine signs. The essential and primordial function of a miracle is either to awaken the grace of Faith—which assumes on the part of the person affected by this grace a natural disposition to admit the supernatural, whether this disposition be conscious or not—or to make perfect a Faith already acquired. To define still more exactly the function of the miracle, not only in Christianity but in all religious forms—for the miraculous is foreign to none of them— it may be said that a miracle, apart from its symbolic character, which links it with the object of Faith itself, is calculated to evoke

---

appears to us an unfathomable mystery, must be lived by us by means of a process whereby, instead of assimilating the mystery to our own mode of understanding, we must on the contrary watch for a profound change, an inward transformation of our spirit, so as to make us fit for the mystical experience" (Vladimir Lossky, *Essai sur la théologie mystique de l'Église d'Orient*).

an intuition that becomes an element of certainty in the soul of the believer. Lastly, if miracles can awaken Faith, Faith can in turn bring about miracles, for "Faith can move mountains." This reciprocal relationship also shows that these two things are connected cosmologically and that there is nothing arbitrary in this connection; thus the miracle establishes an immediate contact between the Divine Omnipotence and the world, while Faith establishes in its turn an analogous but passive contact between the microcosm and God; ordinary ratiocination, that is to say, the discursive operation of the mental faculty, is as far removed from Faith as are natural laws from miracles, while intellectual Knowledge will see the miraculous in the natural and vice versa.

As for Charity, which is the most important of the three theological virtues, it possesses two aspects, one passive and the other active. Spiritual Love is a passive participation in God who is Infinite Love; but merely natural love is, on the contrary, active in relation to created things. Love of one's neighbor, insofar as it is a necessary expression of the Love of God, as an indispensable complement to Faith. These two modes of Charity are affirmed by the Gospel teaching regarding the Supreme Law, the first mode implying consciousness of the fact that God alone is Beatitude and Reality, and the second, consciousness of the fact that the ego is only illusory, the "me" of others being identified in reality with "myself";* if I must love my neighbor because he is "me," this implies that I must love myself a priori, not being other than my neighbor; and if I must love myself, whether in myself or in my neighbor, it is because God loves me and I ought to love what He loves; and if He loves me it is because He loves His creation, or in other words, because Existence itself is Love and Love is as it were the perfume of the Creator inherent in every creature. In the same way that the Love of God, or the Charity that has as its object the Divine Perfections and not our own well-being, is Knowledge of

---

* This realization of the "non-ego" explains the important part played in Christian spirituality by "humility"; a similar part is played in Islamic spirituality by "poverty" (*faqr*) and in Hindu spirituality by "childlikeness" (*bālya*); the symbolism of childhood in the teaching of Christ will be recalled here.

the one and only Divine Reality in which the apparent reality of the creature is dissolved—a knowledge that implies the identification of the soul with its uncreated Essence,* which is yet another aspect of the symbolism of Love—so the love of one's neighbor is basically nothing other than knowledge of the indifferentiation before God of all that is created. Before passing from the created to the Creator, or from manifestation to the Principle, it is in fact necessary to have realized the indifferentiation, or let us say, the nothingness, of all that is manifested. It is toward this that the ethic of Christ is directed, not only by the indistinction that it establishes between the "me" and the "not me," but also, in the second place, by its indifference with regard to individual justification and social equilibrium. Christianity, accordingly by its very nature situates itself outside the "actions and reactions" of the human order; therefore, a priori it is not exoteric. Christian Charity neither has nor can have any interest in "well-being" for its own sake, because true Christianity, like every orthodox religion, considers that the only true happiness human society can enjoy is its spiritual well-being, crowned by the presence of the saint, the goal of every normal civilization; for "the multitude of the wise is the welfare of the world" (Wisd. of Sol. 6:24). One of the truths overlooked by moralists is that when a work of charity is accomplished through love of God, or in virtue of the knowledge that I am the neighbor and that the neighbor is myself—a knowledge that implies this love—the work in question has for the neighbor not only the value of an outward benefit, but also that of a benediction. On the other hand, when charity is exercised neither from love of God nor by virtue of the aforesaid knowledge, but solely with a view to human well-being considered as an end in itself, the benediction inherent in true charity does not accompany the apparent well-doing, either for the giver or for the receiver.

---

* "We are entirely transformed into God," says Meister Eckhart "and changed into Him. Just as, in the sacrament, the bread is changed into the body of Christ, so am I changed into Him, in such wise that He makes me one with His Being and not simply like to it; by the living God, it is true that there is no longer any distinction."

5

The existence of the monastic orders can be explained only by the presence, in the Western as well as the Eastern Church, of an initiatory tradition going back—as St. Benedict and the Hesychasts alike testify—to the Desert Fathers and so to the Apostles and to Christ. The fact that the cenobitism of the Latin Church can be traced back to the same origins as that of the Greek Church—the latter, however, consisting of a single community and not different orders—clearly proves that the first is esoteric in essence like the second; moreover, the eremetical life is considered by both to mark the summit of spiritual perfection—St. Benedict said so expressly in his Rule. Monastic life, far from constituting a self-sufficient way, is described in the Rule of St. Benedict as a "commencement of religious life," while for "him who hastens his steps toward the perfection of monastic life, there are the teachings of the Holy Fathers, the observance of which leads man to the supreme end of religion";* now these are the teachings that form the doctrinal essence of Hesychasm.

According to this doctrine, as in the teachings of every other initiatory tradition, the organ of the spirit, or the principal center of spiritual life, is the heart. But what is more important from the standpoint of spiritual realization is the teaching of Hesychasm on the means of perfecting the natural participation of the human

* We would like to quote the remainder of this passage, which is taken from the last chapter of the book, entitled "That the Practice of Justice Is Not Wholly Contained in This Rule":

What page is there of the Old or New Testament, what divinely authorized word therein, that is not a sure rule for the conduct of man? Again, what book of the holy Catholic Fathers does not resolutely teach us the right road to attain our Creator? Furthermore, what are the Discourses of the Fathers, their Institutions, and their lives [those of the Desert Fathers], and what is the rule of our Father St. Basil, if not a pattern for monks who live and obey as they ought, and authentic records of the virtues? For us who are lax, who lead blameful lives, and are full of negligence, herein is indeed cause to blush with confusion. Whoever then thou mayest be who pressest forward toward the heavenly homeland, accomplish first, with the help of Christ, this poor outline of a rule that we have traced; then at last, with the protection of God, wilt thou reach those sublimer heights of doctrine and virtue the memory of which we have just evoked.

microcosm in the Divine Metacosm by transmuting it into super-natural participation and finally into union and identity: this means consists of the "inward prayer" or "Prayer of Jesus." This Prayer surpasses all the virtues in excellence, for it is a Divine act in us and hence the best of all possible acts. It is only by means of this Prayer that the creature can be really united with his Creator; the goal of the Prayer of Jesus is consequently the supreme spiritual state, in which man is detached from everything pertaining to the creature and, being directly united with the Divinity, is illuminated by the Divine Light. This supreme state is "Holy Silence" ($\dot{\eta}\sigma\nu\chi\dot{\iota}a$), symbolized by the black color of the Virgin in certain icons and images.*

To those who consider the "spiritual prayer" as a simple and even superfluous practice, the Palamite doctrine replies that this prayer represents on the contrary the "straitest" way possible, but that in return it leads to the highest pinnacle of perfection, on con-dition—and this is essential and reduces to nothing the shallow suspicions of moralists—that the activity of prayer be in harmony with all the remainder of one's human activities. In other words, the virtues—or conformity to the Divine Law—constitute the *conditio sine qua non* without which the "spiritual prayer" would be ineffective; we are therefore a long way from the naïve illusion of those who imagine that it is possible to attain the Infinite by means of merely mechanical practices, without any other respon-sibility or obligation. "Virtue," so the Palamite teaching maintains, "disposes us for union with God, but Grace accomplishes this in-expressible union." If the virtues act as modes of knowledge, it is because they retrace by analogy Divine attitudes; there is in fact no

* This "silence" is the exact equivalent of the Hindu and Buddhist *nirvāna* and the Sufic *fanā'* (both terms signifying "extinction"); the "poverty" (*faqr*) in which "union" (*tawhīd*) is achieved refers to the same symbolism. Regard-ing this real union—or this reintegration of the finite in the Infinite—we may also mention the title of a book by St. Gregory Palamas: *Witnesses of the Saints, Showing That Those Who Participate in Divine Grace Become, Comformably with Grace Itself, without Origin and Infinite.* It would be impossible to express the "Supreme Identity" more succinctly than this. We may also recall in this connection the following adage of Moslem esoterism: "The Sufi is not created."

virtue that does not derive from a Divine Prototype, and therein lies their deepest meaning: "to be" is "to know."

Lastly, we must emphasize the fundamental and truly universal significance of the invocation of the Divine Name. This Name, in the Christian form—as in the Buddhist form and in certain branches of the Hindu tradition—is a name of the manifested Word,* in this case the Name of Jesus, which, like every revealed Divine Name when ritually pronounced, is mysteriously identified with the Divinity. It is in the Divine Name that there takes place the mysterious meeting of the created and the Uncreate, the contingent and the Absolute, the finite and the Infinite. The Divine Name is thus a manifestation of the Supreme Principle, or to speak still more plainly, it is the Supreme Principle manifesting Itself; it is not therefore in the first place a manifestation, but the Principle Itself.† "The sun shall be turned into darkness, and the moon into blood, before the great and the terrible day of the Lord come," says the prophet Joel, "but whosoever shall call on the name of the Lord shall be delivered," [3] and we may also recall the beginning of the first Epistle to the Corinthians addressed "to all that in every place call upon the name of Jesus Christ our Lord," and the injunction contained in the first Epistle to the Thessalonians to "unceasing prayer," on which St. John Damascene comments as follows: "We must learn to invoke God's Name more often than we breathe, at all times and everywhere and during all our labors. The Apostle says: Pray without ceasing, which is to say that we must remember God all the time, wherever we are and whatever we are doing."‡ It is not without reason therefore that the Hesy-

---

* We are thinking here of the invocation of Amida Buddha and of the formula *Om mani padme hum,* and as regards Hinduism, of the invocation of Rāma and Krishna.

† Similarly, according to the Christian perspective, Christ is not in the first place man, but God.

‡ In this commentary by St. John Damascene the words "invoke" and "remember" are used to describe or illustrate the same idea; it will be recalled that the Arab word *dhikr* signifies both "invocation" and "remembrance"; in Buddhism also "to think of Buddha" and "to invoke Buddha" are expressed by one and the same word (*Buddhānusmriti;* the Chinese *nien-fo* and the Japanese *nembutsu*). Moreover, it is worth noting that the Hesychasts and the Dervishes use the same word to describe invocation:

chasts consider the invocation of the Name of Jesus as having been bequeathed by Jesus to the Apostles:

It is thus [according to the *Century* of the Monks Callistus and Ignatius] that our merciful and beloved Lord Jesus Christ, at the time when He came to His Passion freely accepted for us, and also at the time when, after His Resurrection, He visibly showed Himself to the Apostles, and even at the moment when He was about to reascend to the Father . . . bequeathed these three things to His disciples [the invocation of His Name, Peace, and Love, which respectively correspond to Faith, Hope, and Charity]. . . . The beginning of all activity of the Divine Love is the confident invocation of the Saving Name of our Lord Jesus Christ, as He Himself said [John 15:5]: "Without me ye can do nothing. . . ." By the confident invocation of the Name of our Lord Jesus Christ, we steadfastly hope to obtain His Mercy and the True Life hidden in Him. It is like unto another Divine Wellspring that is never exhausted [John 4:14] and that yields up these gifts when the Name of our Lord Jesus Christ is invoked, without imperfection, in the heart.

We may also quote the following passage from an Epistle (*Epistola ad Monachos*) of St. John Chrysostom:

I have heard the Fathers say: Who is this monk who forsakes and belittles the rule? He should, when eating and drinking, when seated or serving others, when walking or indeed when doing anything whatsoever, invoke unceasingly: "Lord Jesus Christ, Son of God, have pity on me."* Persevere unceasingly in the Name of our Lord Jesus that

---

the recitation of the Prayer of Jesus is called by the Hesychasts "work," while the Dervishes name every form of invocation "occupation" or "business" (*shughl*).

   * This formula is often contracted to the Name of Jesus alone, particularly by those who are more advanced in the way:

The most important means in the life of prayer is the *Name of God,* invoked in prayer. Ascetics and all who lead a life of prayer, from the anchorites of the Egyptian desert to the Hesychasts of Mount Athos . . . insist above all on the importance of the Name of God. Apart from the Offices there exists for all the Orthodox a "rule of prayer," composed of psalms and different orisons; for monks it is much more considerable. But the most important thing in prayer, the thing that constitutes its very heart, is what is named the Prayer of Jesus: "Lord Jesus Christ, Son of God, have pity on me, a sinner." The repetition of this prayer hundreds of times, and even indefinitely, is the essential element of every monastic rule of prayer; it can, if necessary, replace the Offices and all the other prayers, since its value is universal. The power of the prayer does not reside in its content, which is simple and clear (it is the prayer of the tax-gatherer), but in the

thy heart may drink the Lord and the Lord may drink thy heart, to the end that in this manner the two may become one.

---

sweet Name of Jesus. The ascetics bear witness that this Name contains the power of the Presence of God. Not only is God invoked by this Name—He is already present in the invocation. This can certainly be said of every Name of God; but it is true above all of the Divine and human Name of Jesus, which is the proper Name of God and of man. In short, the Name of Jesus present in the human heart communicates to it the power of deification accorded to us by the Redeemer." [S. Boulgakoff: *L' Orthodoxie*]

The Name of Jesus [says St. Bernard] is not only light, it is also nourishment. All food is too dry to be assimilated by the soul if it is not first sweetened by this condiment; it is too insipid unless this salt seasons its tastelessness. I have no taste for thy writings if I cannot read this Name there; no taste for thy discourse if I do not hear it resounding therein. It is honey for my mouth, melody for my ears, joy for my heart, but it is also a medicine. Does any one among you feel overcome with sadness? Let him then taste Jesus in his mouth and heart, and behold how before the light of His Name all clouds vanish and the sky again becomes serene. Has one among you allowed himself to be led into a fault, and is he experiencing the temptation of despair? Let him invoke the Name of the Life and the Life will restore him." [*Sermons on the Canticle of Canticles*, 15]

Notes

Chapter 3

1. Formalism, which is established for the "average man," allows man to achieve universality. . . . It is in fact the "average man" who is the object of the *Sharī'ah* or sacred law of Islam. . . . The idea of the "average man" establishes a sort of neutrality around each person that guarantees every individuality while obliging everyone to work for all. . . . Islam, as a religion, is the way of unity and totality. Its fundamental dogma is called *At-Tawḥīd,* that is to say, unity or the action of uniting. As a universal religion, it admits of gradations, but each of these gradations is truly Islam in the sense that each and every aspect of Islam reveals the same principles. Its formulas are extremely simple, but the number of its forms is incalculable. The greater the number of these forms, the more perfect is the law. One is a Moslem when one follows one's destiny, that is to say, one's *raison d'être.* . . . The *ex cathedra* utterance of the *mufti* must be clear and comprehensible to all, even to an illiterate Negro. He has no right to make any pronouncement on anything other than the commonplaces of practical life, and in fact never does so, since he is able to avoid questions that do not lie within his competence. It is the clear delimitation, known to all, between Sufic and Sharaite questions that allows Islam to be both esoteric and exoteric without contradicting itself. That is why there are never serious conflicts between science and faith among those Moslems who understand their religion. The formula of *At-Tawḥīd,* or monotheism, is a Sharaite commonplace. The import that a man gives to this formula is his personal affair, since it depends upon his Sufism. Every deduction that one can make from this formula is more or less valid, provided always that it does not destroy the literal meaning; for in that case one destroys the unity of Islam,

that is to say, its universality, its faculty of adapting and fitting itself to all mentalities, circumstances, and epochs. Formalism is indispensable; it is not a superstition but a universal language. Since universality is the principle and the reason for the existence of Islam, and since language is the means of communication between beings endowed with reason, it follows that exoteric formulas are as important in the religious organism as the arteries in the animal body. . . . Life is not divisible; what makes it appear so is that it is capable of gradation. The more the life of the ego identifies itself with the life of the non-ego, the more intensely one lives. The transfusion of the ego into the non-ego is made by means of a gift that is more or less ritual, conscious or voluntary. It will be easily understood that the art of giving is the principal secret of the Great Work. [Abdul-Hādi, "L'universalité en l'Islam," *Le Voile d'Isis,* January, 1934]

Chapter 5

1. When speaking of "Jews, devout men, out of every nation under heaven" (ἀπὸ παντὸς ἔθνους τῶν ὑπὸ τοῦ οὐρανοῦ; *ex omni natione quae sub caelo est*), it is obvious that the Scriptures cannot have the Japanese or the Peruvians in mind, although these people also belong to this terrestrial world that is "under heaven"; moreover, the same text makes clear later on what the authors of the New Testament meant by "every nation under heaven": "We, Parthians and Medes, and Elamites and the dwellers in Mesopotamia and in Judea, and Cappadocia, in Pontus and Asia [Minor], Phrygia, and Pamphylia in Egypt, and in the parts of Libya about Cyrene, and strangers of Rome, Jews and proselytes, Cretans and Arabians, we do hear them speak in our tongues the wonderful works of God" (Acts 2:5–11). The same necessarily restricted conception of the geographical and ethnic world is also implied in these words of Saint Paul: "First, I thank my God through Jesus Christ for you all [of the Church of Rome], that your faith is spoken of throughout the whole world" (ἐν ὅλῳ τῷ κόσμῳ; *in universo mundo*). It is obvious that the author of these words did not mean to imply that the faith of the primitive Church of Rome was known among all peoples who, according to present-day geographical knowledge, make up the "whole world," including, for example, the Mongols or the Aztecs; the "world" was and is, for Christianity, the Western world, with certain extensions into the Near East. When Saint Paul says of the Apostles (Romans 10:18), interpreting two verses of Psalm 19, the sense of which moreover is essentially metaphysical,

that "their sound went into all the earth, and their words unto the ends of the world" (for: "There is no speech nor language, where their voice is not heard. Their line is gone out through all the earth, and their words to the end of the world"), who will accuse him of error or false-hood on the grounds that no Apostle had preached in Siberia or in any other almost inaccessible country, or who will deny that his manner of speaking, since it must have a sense, can only be explained and justified by the necessary and inevitable limitation of every religious "world"? Similarly, when St. Justin Martyr said, a century after Jesus Christ, that there is no human race, whether Greek, Barbarian, or any other, among whom the name of Christ is not invoked, who would think of inter-preting these words literally and of accusing the saint either of false-hood or error? Christ issued the command to "teach all nations" (Matt. 29:19), and it is assumed that this refers to everyone who inhabits the terrestrial globe; but when Christ orders, "Go ye into the world, and preach the gospel to every creature" (Mark 16:15), care is taken not to interpret this literally and preach to every creature without exception, including animals and plants; and especial care is taken to avoid a literal interpretation of the sequel to the same passage, according to which believers are characterized by miraculous gifts such as immunity against poison and power to cure the sick. It is significant, moreover, that the Acts of the Apostles makes no mention whatever of the activities of those Apostles who had moved away from the Roman world; while, on the other hand, Saint Paul and his companion Timothy were "for-bidden of the Holy Ghost to preach the word in Asia," and when they arrived at Mysia and tried to go into Bithynia "the Spirit suffered them not" (Acts 16:6–7).

All these examples indicate in a more or less direct way that for Christianity the Roman world is symbolically and traditionally iden-tified with the whole world, in the same way that for the Chinese Tradition, for example, "the Chinese people" means all humanity; but so far as Christianity is concerned, there is yet another and still more positive indication in support of what we have just said; it is that Christian Rome, the center of the Western Christian world, is heir to Ancient Rome, the center of the Roman world, and that the pope, at least as "Supreme Pontiff" (*pontifex maximus*), is heir to the Roman emperor; and let us not forget that Christ, in saying, "Give unto Caesar those things which are Caesar's," recognized and as it were consecrated the traditional legitimacy of the emperor.

Chapter 8

1. We may also quote a contemporary Catholic author, Paul Vulliaud:

We have put forward the view that the process of dogmatic enunciation during the first centuries was one of successive Initiation, or in a word, that there existed an exoterism and an esoterism in the Christian religion. Historians may not like it, but one finds incontestable traces of the *lex arcani* at the origin of our religion. . . . In order to grasp quite clearly the doctrinal teaching of the Christian Revelation, it is necessary to admit, as we have already insisted, the twofold nature of the gospel preaching. The rule enjoining that the dogmas should be revealed only to Initiates continued in operation long enough to enable even the blindest and most refractory observers to detect undeniable traces of it. Sozoma, a historian, wrote concerning the Council of Nicaea that he wished to record it in detail, primarily "in order to leave for posterity a public monument of truth." He was advised to remain silent concerning "that which must not be known except by priests and the faithful." The "law of the secret" was in consequence perpetuated, in certain places, even after the universal conciliar divulgation of the Dogma. . . . Saint Basil, in his work *On the True and Pious Faith,* relates how he avoided making use of terms, such as Trinity and consubstantiality, that, as he said, do not occur in the Scriptures, although the things that they denote are to be found there. . . . Tertullian says, opposing Praxeas, that one should not speak in so many words of the Divinity of Jesus Christ, and that one should call the Father "God" and the Son "Lord." . . . Do not such locutions, practiced habitually, seem like the signs of a convention, since this reticence of language is found in all the authors of the first centuries and is of canonical application? The primitive discipline of Christianity included an examination at which the *competent* [those who asked for baptism] were admitted to election. This examination was called the scrutiny. The Sign of the Cross was made on the ears of the catechumen with the word *Ephpheta,* for which reason this ceremony came to be called "the scrutiny of the opening of the ears." The ears were opened to the *reception* [*cabālāh*] or *tradition* of the Divine truths. . . . The Synoptico-Johannine problem . . . cannot be resolved except by recalling the existence of a twofold teaching, exoteric and acroamatic, historical and theologico-mystical. . . . There is a parabolic theology. It formed part of that inheritance that Theodoret calls, in the preface to his *Commentary on the Song of Songs,* the "paternal inheritance," which signifies the transmission of the meaning applicable to the interpretation of the Scriptures. . . . The Dogma, in its divine part, constituted the revelation reserved to the Initiates, under the "Discipline of the Secret." Tentzelius claimed to have traced back the origin of this "law of the secret" to the end of the second century. . . . Emmanuel Schelstrate, librarian of the Vatican, rightly noted it in apostolic times. In reality, the esoteric manner of transmitting Divine truths and interpreting texts existed among both Jews and Gentiles, as it later existed among Christians . . . If one obstinately refuses to study the initiatory methods of Revelation, one will never arrive at an intelligent subjective assimilation of the Dogma. The ancient Liturgies are not sufficiently put to use, and in the same way Hebrew scholarship is absolutely neglected. . . . The Apostles and the Fathers have preserved in secret and silence the "Majesty of the Mysteries," St. Denys the Areopagite has of set purpose cultivated the use of obscure words; as Christ assumed the title "Son of Man," so he calls baptism "Initiation to Theogenesis." . . . The discipline of the secret was fully justified. Neither the Prophets nor Christ Himself revealed the Divine Secrets with such clearness as to make them comprehensible to all." [Paul Vulliaud, *Études d'ésotérisme catholique*]

Lastly we should like to quote, for the sake of documentation and despite the length of the text, an author of the early nineteenth century:

In the beginning Christianity was an initiation comparable to those of the pagans. When speaking of this religion Clement of Alexandria exclaims: "O truly sacred mysteries! O pure light! Amid the gleam of torches falls the veil that covers God and Heaven. I become holy from the moment I am *initiated*. It is the Lord Himself who is the hierophant; He sets His *seal* upon the adept whom He enlightens; and to reward his faith he commends him eternally to His Father. Those are the orgies of my mysteries. *Come and seek admission to them*." These words might be taken in a merely metaphorical sense, but the facts prove that they must be interpreted literally. The Gospels are full of calculated reticences and of allusions to Christian initiation. Thus one may read: "he who hath ears, let him hear." Jesus, when addressing the multitude, always made use of parables. "Seek," he said, "and ye shall find; knock, and it shall be opened unto you." The meetings were in secret and people were admitted only under stated conditions. Complete understanding of the doctrine was achieved only after passing through three grades of instruction. The Initiates were consequently divided into three classes. The first class comprised the *hearers,* the second the *catechumens* or the *competent,* and the third the *faithful.* The hearers were novices, who were prepared, by means of certain practices and instructions, for the communication of the dogmas of Christianity. A portion of these dogmas was disclosed to the catechumens, who, after the prescribed purifications, received baptism or "Initiation to Theogenesis" [divine generation], as St. Denys calls it in his *Ecclesiastical Hierarchy;* from that time onward they became *servants of the faith* and had free access to the churches. In the mysteries there was nothing secret or hidden from the faithful; all was accomplished in their presence; they could see all and hear all; they had the right to be present during the whole liturgy; it was enjoined upon them that they should watch attentively lest any profane person or initiate of inferior rank should slip in among them; and the *sign of the cross* served them as a sign of recognition. The mysteries were divided into two parts. The first was called the "Mass of the Catechumens," because members of that class were allowed to attend it; it included all that is said from the beginning of the Divine Office up to the recitation of the Creed. The second part was called the "Mass of the Faithful." It included the preparation of the *sacrifice,* the sacrifice itself, and the giving of thanks that follows. When this Mass was about to begin, a deacon cried in a loud voice: *Sancta sanctis; foris canes;* "The holy things are for the holy; let the dogs go out!" Thereupon they expelled the catechumens and the penitents, the latter being members of the faithful who, being guilty of some serious offense, had been subjected to the penances prescribed by the Church, and thus were unable to be present at the celebration of the "awful mysteries," as St. John Chrysostom calls them. The faithful, once alone, recited the symbol of the faith, in order to ensure that all present had received initiation and so that one might safely hold converse before them *openly and without enigmas* concerning the great mysteries of the religion and especially of the Eucharist. The doctrine and the celebration of this sacrament was guarded as an inviolable secret; and if the doctors referred to it in their sermons or books, they did so only with great reserve, by indirect allusion and enigmatically. When Diocletian ordered the Christians to deliver their sacred books to the magistrates, those among them who obeyed this edict of the Emperor from fear of death were driven out of the community of the faithful and were looked upon as traitors and apostates. St. Augustine gives us some idea of the grief of the Church at seeing the sacred Scriptures handed over to unbelievers. In the eyes of the Church it was regarded as a terrible profanation when a man who had not been initiated entered the temple and witnessed the holy mysteries. St. John Chrysostom mentions a case of this kind to Pope Innocent I. Some barbarian soldiers had entered the Church of Constantinople on Easter Eve. "The female catechumens, who had just undressed in order to be baptized, were compelled by fear to flee in a state of nakedness; the barbarians did not allow them time to cover themselves. The barbarians then entered the places where the sacred things are kept and venerated, and some of them, *who had not yet been initiated into our mysteries,* saw all the most sacred things that were there." In the seventh century, the constant increase in the number of the faithful led to the institution by the Church of the minor orders, among which were numbered the *porters,* who succeeded the deacons and subdeacons in the duty of guarding the doors of the churches. About the year 700, everyone was admitted to the spectacle of the liturgy, and of all the mystery that in early times surrounded the sacred ceremonial, there remained only the custom of reciting secretly the Canon of the Mass. Nevertheless, even today, in the Greek rite, the officiating priest celebrates the Divine Office behind a curtain, which is drawn back only at the moment of the Elevation; but at this moment those assisting should be prostrated or bowed in such a manner that they cannot see the Blessed Sacrament." [F. T. B. Clavel, *Histoire pittoresque de la Franc-Maçonnerie et des sociétés secrètes anciennes et modernes*]

2. A distinction analogous to the one that sets in opposition Faith and the Law is to be found within the initiatory realm itself; to Faith correspond here the various spiritual movements founded upon the invocation of a Divine Name (the Hindu *japa,* the Buddhist *buddhā-nusmriti, nien-fo,* or *nembutsu,* and the Moslem *dhikr;* a particularly characteristic example is provided by Shrī Chaitanya, who threw away all his books in order to devote himself exclusively to the "bhaktic" invocation of Krishna, an attitude comparable to that of the Christians who rejected the Law and "works" in the name of Faith and Love. Similarly, to cite yet another example, the Japanese Buddhist schools called *Jōdo* and *Jōdo Shin,* whose doctrine, founded on the sutras of Amitābha, is analogous to certain doctrines of Chinese Buddhism and proceeds, like them, from the "original vow of Amida," reject the meditations and austerities of the other Buddhist schools in order to devote themselves exclusively to the invocation of the sacred Name of Amida: here ascetic effort is replaced by simple confidence in the Grace of the Buddha Amida, a grace that He bestows out of His compassion on those who invoke Him, independently of any merit on their part.

The invocation of the holy Name must be accompanied by an absolute sincerity of heart and the most complete faith in the goodness of Amida, whose will it is that all creatures should be saved. In place of virtues, in place of knowledge, Amida, taking pity on the men of the "Latter Days," has allowed that there be substituted faith in the redemptive value of His Grace, in order that they may be delivered from the sufferings of the world.

We are all equal by the effect of our common faith and of our confidence in the Grace of Amida Buddha.

Every creature, however great a sinner he may be, is certain of being saved and enfolded in the light of Amida and of obtaining a place in the eternal and imperishable Land of Happiness, if only he believes in the Name of

Amida Buddha and, abandoning the present and future cares of the world, takes refuge in the liberating Hands so mercifully stretched out toward all creatures, reciting His Name with an entire sincerity of heart.

We know the Name of Amida through the preaching of Shakyamuni, and we know that included in this Name is the strength of Amida's desire to save all creatures. To hear this Name is to hear the voice of Salvation saying, "Have confidence in Me and I shall surely save you," words that Amida addresses to us directly. This meaning is contained in the Name "Amida." Whereas all our other actions are more or less stained with impurity, the repetition of the *Namu-Amida-Bu* is an act devoid of all impurity, for it is not we who recite it but Amida Himself who, giving us His own Name, makes us repeat It.

When once belief in our salvation by Amida has been awakened and strengthened, our destiny is fixed: we shall be reborn in the Pure Land and shall become Buddhas. Then, it is said, we shall be entirely enfolded in the Light of Amida and living under His loving direction, our life will be filled with joy unspeakable, gift of the Buddha.

[From *Les Sectes bouddhiques japonaises*
by E. Steinilber-Oberlin and Kuni Matsuo]

The original vow of Amida is to receive in his Land of Felicity whoever shall pronounce His Name with absolute confidence: happy then are those who pronounce His Name! A man may possess faith, but if he does not pronounce the Name his faith will be of no use to him. Another may pronounce the Name while thinking of that alone, but if his faith is not sufficiently deep, his re-birth will not take place. But he who believes firmly in re-birth as the goal of *nembutsu* [invocation] and who pronounces the Name, the same will without any doubt be reborn in the Land of Reward.

[From *Essays in Zen Buddhism,* vol. 2, by D. T. Suzuki]

3. The Psalms contain a number of references to the invocation of the Name of God:

I have cried to the Lord with my voice: and he hath heard me from his holy hill.

And I have called upon the name of the Lord. O Lord, deliver my soul.

The Lord is nigh unto all them that call upon him, to all that call upon him in truth.

Two passages also contain a reference to the Eucharistic mode of invocation:

Open thy mouth wide, and I will fill it.

Who satisfieth thy mouth with good things, so that thy youth is renewed like the eagle's.

So also Isaiah:

Fear not: for I have redeemed thee, I have called thee by thy name; thou art mine.

Seek ye the Lord while he may be found, call ye upon him while he is near.

And so Solomon in the Book of Wisdom:

I called upon God, and the spirit of wisdom came upon me.

The verse from the prophet Joel quoted above situates the rite of invocation within a framework of conditions that are those obtaining at the end of the Dark Age (the Hindu *Kali-yuga*), but that also characterize, when considering the four ages taken together (the *mahā-yuga*), the Dark Age as a whole. Now, according to the *Vishnu-Dharma-Uttara*,

that which is obtained by meditation in the age of *Krita*, by sacrifice in the age of *Trēta*, by devotion in the age of *Dwāpara*, is obtained in the *Kali* age by celebrating Keshava [Vishnu].

The repetition of His Name, O Maitreya, is for faults the equivalent of fire for metals.

Water suffices to put out fire, the sunrise to disperse the darkness; in the *Kali* age the repetition of the Name of Hari [Vishnu] suffices to destroy all errors.

Again, the *Mānava-Dharma-Shāstra* says:

There is no doubt that a Brahmin can attain to Beatitude by invocation alone.

Here are some analogous Buddhist texts:

In the present age, which belongs to the fourth half-millennium after Buddha, what we have to do is to repent of our transgressions, cultivate the virtues, and pronounce the Name of Buddha. Is it not said that to think of the Buddha Amitābha and to pronounce His Name . . . purifies us of all transgressions committed by us in all our lives during eighty thousand million *kalpas?*

The devotee must utter without interruption [St. Paul says, "Pray without ceasing"] the Name of Buddha with one sole thought, leaving no room in his mind for anything else, and he is then sure to be reborn in the presence of Buddha."

[Tao Ch'ao, a Chinese Master]

Because beings endowed with sensible faculties meet many obstacles in their road, and the world in which they live is full of subtle temptations; because (in the present age or latter days, and above all as the end of this epoch draws near) their thoughts are too perplexed, their intelligence too clumsy, and their minds too distraught . . . , taking pity on them, Buddha counsels them to concentrate on the recitation of His Name, for when it is practised without interruption, the devotee is certain to be reborn in the Land of Amida.

[Shan Tao, a Chinese Master]

For one who is absorbed in the Name of Buddha, which is above time, there is a rebirth which knows neither beginning nor end.

There is only the Name of Buddha and outside it exists neither he who utters it nor he to whom it is uttered. There is only the Name of Buddha and outside it there is no rebirth. All things that exist are virtues included in the body of the Name of Buddha itself. . . . It is better to be possessed by the Name than to possess the Name. All things are of one spirit, but this spirit is not manifested by Itself. The eye cannot see itself . . . but hold a mirror in front of you and the eye will be able to see itself, such is the virtue of the mirror. And the mirror is one that each one of us possesses and that is called the great mirror of illumination; it is the Name already realized by all the Buddhas.

[Ippen, a Japanese Master; see
D. T. Suzuki, *Essays in Zen Buddhism*]

Regarding the Hindu *japa,* and indeed invocation in general, instructive observations may be found in the teachings of Shrī Ramakrishna.

The following is a selection of quotations from the numerous verses of the Koran referring to invocation:

Remember Me, and I will remember you.

To Allāh belong the most beautiful Names: call on Him by them!

O Believers! when you are face to face with an armed troop, be resolute and repeat without ceasing the name of Allāh, that you may prosper.

Allāh leads to Himself all those who turn to Him, who believe in Him, and whose hearts have rest in the invocation of Allāh; is it not by the invocation of Allāh that hearts find rest?

Who speaks a better word than he who calls upon Allāh?

Your Lord has said: Call Me and I will answer you.

It is certain that the invocation of Allāh is of all things the greatest.

The following *aḥādīth* of the Prophet may also be cited:

Whenever men gather together to invoke Allāh, they are surrounded by Angels, the Divine Favor envelops them, and Peace [*Sakīnah*] descends upon them, and Allāh remembers them in His assembly.

There is a means of polishing all things whereby rust may be removed; that which polishes the heart is the invocation of Allāh, and there is no act that removes the punishment of Allāh further from you than this invocation. The Companions said: Is not the battle against unbelievers equal to it? The Prophet replied: No, not even if you fight on until your sword is shattered.

Index